101 Best Sex Scenes Ever Written

Other books by Barnaby Conrad

"101 Best" Series for Writers
101 Best Scenes Ever Written
101 Best Beginnings Ever Written

Other Nonfiction
La Fiesta Brava
Gates of Fear
Death of Manolete
San Francisco: A Profile in Words and Pictures
Famous Last Words
Tahiti
Encyclopedia of Bullfighting
How to Fight a Bull
Fun While It Lasted
A Revolting Transaction
Time Is All We Have
Hemingway's Spain
The Complete Guide to Writing Fiction
Name Dropping
Snoopy's Guide to the Writing Life (with Monte Schulz)
The World of Herb Caen
Learning to Write Fiction from the Masters
Santa Barbara

Fiction
The Innocent Villa
Matador
Dangerfield
Zorro: A Fox in the City
Endangered (with Niels Mortensen)
Fire Below Zero (with Nico Mastorakis)
Keepers of the Secret (with Nico Mastorakis)
Last Boat to Cadiz
The Second Life of John Wilkes Booth

Translations
The Wounds of Hunger (Spota)
The Second Life of Captain Contreras (Luca de Tena)
My Life as a Matador (Autobiography of Carlos Arruza)

101 Best Sex Scenes Ever Written

An Erotic Romp Through Literature
for Writers and Readers

Barnaby Conrad

Quill
Driver
Books

Fresno, California

Published by Quill Driver Books
an imprint of Linden Publishing
2006 South Mary, Fresno, California 93721
559-233-6633 / 800-345-4447
QuillDriverBooks.com

Quill Driver Books and Colophon are trademarks of
Linden Publishing, Inc.

ISBN 978-1-610350-01-3

135798642

Printed in the United States of America
on acid-free paper.

Library of Congress Cataloging-in-Publication Data

Conrad, Barnaby, 1922-
  101 best sex scenes ever written : an erotic romp through literature for writers and readers / Barnaby Conrad.
      p. cm.
  Includes index.
  ISBN 978-1-61035-001-3 (pbk. : alk. paper)
  1. Erotic stories--Authorship. 2. Erotic stories--Technique. 3.
Sex in literature. I. Title. II. Title: One hundred one best sex scenes
ever written. III. Title: One hundred and one best sex scenes ever
written. IV. Title: Best sex scenes ever written. V. Title: Erotic
romp through literature for writers and readers.
  PN3377.5.E76C66 2011
  809.3'93543--dc22
                                          2011008201

"The dirtiest book of all is an expurgated book."
Walt Whitman

Among the authors whose writing is quoted in this book
are the following:

Saul Bellow, Anthony Burgess, James M. Cain, Michael Chabon, Peter De Vries, Nelson DeMille, William Faulkner, Gustave Flaubert, Ken Follett, Graham Greene, Ernest Hemingway, James Jones, Elmore Leonard, Sinclar Lewis, John D. MacDonald, Peter Mathiessen, Somerset Maugham, Henry Miller, Margaret Mitchell, Toni Morrison, Vladimir Nabokov, Anäis Nin, John O'Hara, Joyce Carol Oates, Robert B. Parker, Nora Roberts, Philip Roth, Jane Smiley, Betty Smith, Susan Sontag, Danielle Steele, John Steinbeck, William Styron, Paul Theroux, John Updike, Joan Wickersham,

and many more.

"Literature is all—or mostly—about sex."
Anthony Burgess

Contents

Introduction

"Sex is God's joke on human beings."
Bette Davis

SINCE SEX IS MANKIND'S OLDEST—AND MOST IMPORTANT—PASTIME, it is not strange that so much has been written about it since writing began.

What *is* remarkable is that, in light of the fact that there are a very limited number of orifices and appendages associated with the human body, there seems to be no limit to what amalgamations and problems and comeuppances the creative mind can conceive of when dealing with and writing about most this ancient and most basic activity.

W. H. Auden maintained that no two people ever read the same book. Perhaps we can expand Auden's thought by saying that no two people ever got the same reaction from the same sex scene.

Not so long ago, the author and publisher of this book would have been jailed for propagating pornography. In 1944, for example, Lillian Smith's acclaimed novel, *Strange Fruit*, was banned in Massachusetts because of the author's onetime use of a four-letter word in a pivotal scene, a word known and dear to most school kids in the country.

Hard to believe now, but when Lucille Ball wanted to tell her TV fans that she was going to have a baby, she wasn't allowed to say the word "pregnant" on the air but was obliged to use the Spanish word, *encinta*.

As author Bill Bryson wrote in his book *Made in America* about the *Strange Fruit* case:

The publishers took the state to court, but the case fell apart when the defense attorney arguing for its sale was unable to bring himself to utter the objectionable word in court, in effect conceding that it was too filthy for public consumption. "In 1948, Norman Mailer caused a sensation by including *pissed off* in *The Naked and the Dead*. Three years later, America got its first novel to use four-letter words extensively when James Jones's *From Here to Eternity* was published. Even there the editors were at sixes and sevens over which words to allow. They allowed *fuck* and *shit* (though not without excising about half of such appearances from the original manuscript) but drew the line at *cunt* and *prick*."

Against such a background, dictionary makers became seized with uncertainty. In the 1960s, the Merriam Webster *Third New International Dictionary* broke new ground by including a number of taboo words—*cunt, shit*, and *prick*—but lost its nerve when it came to *fuck*. Mario Pei protested the omission in the *New York Times*, but of course without being able to specify what the word was. To this day, America remains to an extraordinary degree a land of euphemism. Even now the U.S. State Department cannot bring itself to use the word *prostitute*. Instead it refers to "available casual indigenous female companions."

Many American newspapers had never used the word penis until Mrs. Lorena Bobbitt bobbed her husband's in his sleep, and the press was forced to call, well, a spade a spade. (What a wonderful scene it would make in a novel or film when the first persons spotted the dismembered member after it was tossed out of the car by Lorena: "Listen, Lucinda, I know I've had a couple of drinks but would you mind lookin' over here—yeah, there in the grass there—is that what I think it is?" And Lucinda says, "Oh God—poor Johnny Bobbitt!")

What exactly is obscenity's definition? Not until 1957 did the Supreme Court get around to considering the matter of obscenity, and then it was unable to make any more penetrating judgment than that it was material that appealed to "prurient interests" and inflamed "lustful thoughts." In effect, it ruled that obscenity could be recognized but not defined—or as Justice Potter Stewart famously put it: "I know it when I see it."

Justice Stewart surely would label this book pure porn, and of course, considered out of context, many of the scenes read as though they were, indeed, porn. Yet every excerpt is from a distinguished writer, often a great one, and its source is a published and respected novel or short story. You will read scenes from the writings of five Nobel Prize winners and many Pulitzer Prize authors. What surprised me was how surprised people have been when I tell them that some of the most graphic "encounters" in the book came from books they wouldn't have expected, eliciting, for example: "Why, I didn't even remember that multi-paged sex scene in *Sophie's Choice!*"

The selections were not chosen gratuitously, not included to titillate—(sorry)—the reader. They all advanced the plot in some way or helped to characterize the protagonists of the story they came from.

"Action is character," Scott Fitzgerald said, and certainly sex is action, no matter how it is modified: shyly, reluctantly, occasionally, frantically, often, seldom, vigorously, mechanically, lovingly, desperately, routinely, expertly, clumsily, *ad adverbium infinitum.*

All those adverbs, the different ways to describe "it," are one of the reasons we are attracted to what the late William F. Buckley, Jr. called "the OSS," the obligatory sex scene.

In 1525, one Pietro Aretino published "16 Modi, or Ways of Copulation," with sonnets to match.

This book is not intended to be a handbook for those ways, or the definitive book on the writings of sex throughout the ages; I shall leave such works as *The Kama Sutra, Catullus,*the tales of Rabelais and Balzac, *Fanny Hill,* Zola's *Nana, The Story Of O, Moll Flanders, Maggie, A Girl Of The Streets,* Molly Bloom's famous soliloquy, etcetera, for the scholars and porn mavens to analyze, while I take on the cases of more modern dramatic interest. I shan't even include Chaucer's famous "The Miller's Tale" from *The Canterbury Tale,* since it seems more like a crude sophomoric joke than a sex scene. (Joan Acocella, in a recent *New Yorker* article, remarked that "it ('The Miller's Tale') involves an act of involuntary cunnilingus—a rare event, surely.")

In the following pages, I'll be concerned with heterosexual scenes from the more modern approach to this universal pastime. I shall leave the literature of same sex and kinky sex and bestiality to those who see drama or purpose or exemplary behavior therein.

A recent letter from the author Anthony Weller, contained the following right-on thoughts:

I would argue that what makes a sex scene "work" is a balance between its eroticism and its language. When either overwhelms the other (or when the scene's character and tone depart from those of the book as a whole), you have either, on the one hand, pornography, or, artificial writing. But this is, of course, in the eye of the beholder. Many find John Updike a great sensual poet; I can't get past feeling him trying hard for a good grade, while his sentences primp and preen in a mirror.

I'd add only that there are books whose raciness depends on what age you are when you first encounter them. For example, the 007 thrillers, read by me at age eleven or so, seemed impossibly racy and exciting at the time; now they don't. I suspect it's not because they seem less risqué four decades later, but rather because I'm grown up and they no longer offer me a view of a hitherto unseen adult world. Maybe.

Of course, I hope the average reader will enjoy this book, but I trust that it will be truly important to help the beginning writer of fiction when he or she comes to that daunting and necessary sex scene.

How to phrase it? How to describe this most private of human acts? Which are the appropriate words for such soul-bearing behavior? Do I use the anatomically correct words, or the hundreds of common vulgarities? Or, do I just hint at all that happens in the bedroom or in the back of a car or in the attic and leave all of the "dirty stuff" up to the reader? How did my favorite author describe them? Just how graphically did he or she present the scene? Do I want to go the same route?

So let us get started. We will begin with a bang. Or, rather, we won't. Instead, we'll commence with the sexiest scene ever written, from the book which has often been called "the first truly realistic novel."

You don't have to buckle your seat belt for this one; *you* are going to be the reader—and the writer!

1

The Best

———

"No woman ever loved a eunuch."
Gustave Flaubert

IT IS DIFFICULT TO BELIEVE THAT THIS HARD-HITTING, MODERN NOVEL, by Gustave Flaubert, was written way back in 1857. *Madame Bovary* caused a furor because of its total frankness in picturing the life of an adulteress.

Emma, the beautiful daughter of a farmer, is taken in marriage by Charles Bovary, a doctor and widower. He adores her, but she is bored by him and dreams of a real romance. She has a clandestine affair with Rodolphe, a wealthy womanizer, who soon dumps her. Her real heart throb is the decent young law clerk, Leon Dupuis, who lusts after her, but their love is not consummated, and he leaves town.

Then one day she goes to Rouen to the theater and happens to bump into Leon in front of the church. The following famous scene takes place:

An urchin was playing in the square: "Boy, get me a cab!"

The youngster vanished like a shot up the Rue des Quatre-Vents, and for a few minutes they were left alone, face to face and a little embarrassed.

"Oh, Leon…Really…I don't know… whether I should…!" she said, a little coyly. Then, putting on a serious tone:

"It's very improper, you know."

"What's improper about it?" retorted the clerk. "Everybody does it in Paris!"

It was an irresistible and clinching argument.

But there was no sign of a cab. Leon was terrified that she'd retreat back into the church.

Finally the cab appeared.

"Drive past the north door, at least!" the verger urged from the entrance as they went to the coach. "Take a look at the Resurrection, the Last Judgment, Paradise, King David, and the souls of the damned in the flames of hell!"

"Where does Monsieur wish to go?" asked the coachman.

"Anywhere!" said Leon, pushing Emma into the carriage.

And the lumbering contraption rolled away.

It went down the Rue Grand-Pont, crossed the Place des Arts, the Quai Napoleon, and the Pont Neuf, and stopped in front of the statue of Pierre Corneille.

"Keep going!" called a voice from within.

It started off again, and gathering speed on the downgrade beyond the Carrefour Lafayette, it came galloping up to the railway station.

"No! Straight on!" gasped the same voice.

Rattling out through the station gates, the cab soon turned into the boulevard, where it proceeded at a gentle trot between the double row of tall elms. The coachman wiped his brow, stowed his leather hat between his legs, and veered the cab off beyond the side lanes to the grass strip along the river front.

It continued along the river on the cobbled towing path for a long time in the direction of Oyssel, leaving the islands behind.

But suddenly it rushed off through Quatre-Mares, Sotteville, the Grande-Chaussee, the Rue d'Elbeuf, and made its third stop— this time at the Jardin des Plantes.

"Get going!" cried the voice, more furiously.

And starting off again, it went through Saint-Sever, along the Quai des Curandiers and the Quai aux Meules, recrossed the bridge, crossed the Place du Champ-de-Mars and continued on behind the garden of the hospital, where old men in black jackets were strolling in the sun on a terrace green with ivy; it went up the

Boulevard Bouvreuil, along the Boulevard Cauchoise, and traversed Mont-Riboudet as far as the hill at Deville.

There it turned back, and from then on it wandered at random, with no apparent goal. It was seen at Saint-Pol, at Lescure, at Mont-Gargan, at Rouge-Mare and the Place du Gaillardbois; in the Rue Maladrerie, the Rue Dinanderie, and in front of one church after another—Saint-Romain, Saint-Vivien, Saint-Maclou, Saint-Nicaise; in front of the customs house, at the Basse Vieille-Tour, at Trois-Pipes, and at the Cimetiere Monumental. From his seat the coachman now and again cast longing glances at a café. He couldn't imagine what restless craving for movement was making these people persist in refusing to stop. He tried a few times, only to hear immediate angry exclamations from behind. So he lashed anew at his two sweating nags, and paid no attention whatever to bumps in the road; he ran into things right and left, past caring—demoralized, and almost weeping with thirst, fatigue, and despair.

Along the river from amidst the wagons and the barrels, along the streets, the bourgeois on the corners stared wide-eyed at this unheard of spectacle—a carriage with drawn blinds that kept appearing and reappearing, sealed tighter than a tomb and tossing like a ship.

At a certain moment in the early afternoon, when the sun was blazing down most fiercely on the old silver-plated lamps, a bare hand appeared from under the little yellow cloth curtains and threw out some torn scraps of paper. The wind caught them and scattered them, and they alighted at a distance, like white butterflies, on a field of flowering red clover.

Finally, at about six o'clock, the carriage stopped in a side street near the Place Beauvoisine. A woman got out and walked off, her veil down, without a backward glance.

(Interesting footnote: A year after the publication of the novel, cabs in Hamburg, Germany, could be rented for sexual dalliance; they were known as "Bovaries.")

Why is this scene of Flaubert's considered by many people to be the best sex scene ever written?

Because the reader does all the work—he, or she, creates what happens in the carriage in his or her own mind, proving once again that the most powerful sex organ can be found between the ears.

It would be an interesting experiment to invite five female writers and five male writers to each give us a chapter about exactly what went on inside that vehicle. They might all come to the same conclusion, but in ten very different ways.

Flaubert's attitude toward the writing about sex in novels was far ahead of its time. In 1852, he wrote to his friend Louise Colet indignantly about a popular novel he'd read by Lamartine:

And first of all, to put the matter bluntly, does he fuck her or doesn't he? The pair of them aren't human beings, they're mannequins. How beautiful these love stories are where the principal thing is so surrounded by mystery that one doesn't know what in the world is going on, sexual intercourse being systematically relegated to the shadow along with drinking, eating, pissing, etc! This partiality irritates me no end. Here's a strapping young fellow who is living with a woman who loves him and whom he loves, and never a desire! Not a single impure cloud ever appears to darken this pale blue lake! Had he told the real story, it would have been even more beautiful! But truth demands hairier males than Monsieur de Lamartine. It is easier in fact to draw an angel than a woman: the wings hide the hunched back.

In his book *The Perpetual Orgy,* the Peruvian novelist Mario Vargas Llosa echoes the same sentiment 150 years after Flaubert:

I have very often had precisely the same reaction to a story: a novel that leaves out sexual experience annoys me as much as one that reduces life exclusively to sexual experience (although the latter irritates me less than the former; I have already said that among forms of unreality I prefer the most concrete one). I need to know whether the hero excites the heroine (and vice versa), and in order for these protagonists to seem lifelike to me, it is indispensable that I be caught up in their mutual excitement. The treatment of sex constitutes one of the most delicate problems in fiction; along with politics it is perhaps the most difficult subject of all to deal with.

Later, Flaubert wrote to Louise: "The good old sex organ is the basis of human affection; it is not itself affection, but rather it's *substratum*, as philosophers would say. No woman has ever loved a eunuch."

And dear old Arthur Schopenhauer, the German pessimist philosopher, chimes in with:

"The organs of sex are the seat of the will."

2

Off Camera

"I won't write about sex until my mother dies."
William Saroyan

IN MOVIE PARLANCE, THE *MADAME BOVARY* SEX SCENE TOOK PLACE "off camera." The audience didn't *see* what actually happened in the coach—because the author so wisely chose not to tell us.

In a similar fashion, James M. Cain in his 1934 blockbuster, *The Postman Always Rings Twice*, treats the sex scene almost as subtly.

"They threw me off the hay truck at noon," is the novel's first sentence.

Frank Chambers is a twenty-four-year-old drifter who lands a job at a "roadside sandwich joint, like a million others in California," run by Nick Papadakis and his tough, hormonal young wife, Cora:

> Except for the shape, she really wasn't any raving beauty, but she had a silky look to her, and her lips stuck out in a way that made me want to mash them in for her.

Within a short time, Frank and Cora are lovers. In Chapter 3, we learn something of Cora's character, background, and the fact that she is up to no good; in fact, she is hinting at murdering her husband.

> "Look out, Frank. You'll break a spring leaf."
> "To hell with the spring leaf."

We were crashing into a little eucalyptus grove beside the road. The Greek had sent us down to the market to take back some T-bone steaks he said were lousy, and on the way back it had got dark. I slammed the car in there, and it bucked and bounced, but when I was in among the trees I stopped. Her arms were around me before I even cut the lights. We did plenty. After a while we just sat there. "I can't go on like this, Frank."

"Me neither."

Does the reader need any more than:

"We did plenty"?

Most people have *done plenty* in a car at one time or another and can easily fill in the blanks.

Off-camera sex was the norm in most early novels. Daringly, the man and woman would usually disappear into the woods or a bedroom, several asterisks would appear, and nine months later she would have a baby and a problem. We certainly don't "see" any actual sex in books like *The Scarlet Letter,* Nathaniel Hawthorne's classic 1850 novel about Hester Prynne and her conviction for adultery.

Similarly, we don't "see" the sex in Somerset Maugham's "Sadie Thompson," a tale about a prostitute, which was made into the 1922 play *Rain,* and into subsequent films. (Both ladies were done in by ministers.) Sex is the total reason for the story, but we don't actually witness any.

Maugham has a lovely story called "The Treasure*"* which is totally built around one sex scene, and in which, again, the reader again isn't allowed to see any actual sex action. Does he miss every detail—or any detail? I don't think so.

In Maugham's story, Richard Harenger, a distinguished, proper, and wealthy London bachelor, hires Pritchard, a comely younger woman, as his housekeeper. For four years, she is the perfect servant and he is always the aloof employer. Then one night, when he is feeling lonely, on an impulse he invites her to a film. Afterwards, they go to a restaurant, and he asks her to dance.

"Why, you dance perfectly, Pritchard," he said.
"It's coming back to me."

Although she was a big woman, she was light on her feet, and she had a natural sense of rhythm. She was very pleasant to dance with. He gave a glance at the mirrors that lined the walls, and he could not help reflecting that they looked very well together. Their eyes met in the mirror; he wondered whether she was thinking that, too. They had two more dances, and then Richard Harenger suggested that they should go. He paid the bill and they walked out. He noticed that she threaded her way through the crowd without a trace of self-consciousness. They got into a taxi and in ten minutes were at home.

"I'll go up the back way, sir," said Pritchard.

"There's no need to do that. Come up in the lift with me."

He took her up, giving the night porter an icy glance, so that he should not think it strange that he came back at the somewhat late hour with his parlormaid, and with his latchkey let her into the flat.

"Well, good night, sir," she said. "Thank you very much. It's been a real treat for me."

"Thank you, Pritchard. I should have had a very dull evening by myself. I hope you've enjoyed your outing."

"That I have, sir, more than I can say."

It had been a success. Richard Harenger was satisfied with himself. It was a kindly thing for him to have done. It was a very agreeable sensation to give anyone so much real pleasure. His benevolence warmed him and for a moment he felt a great love in his heart to the whole human race.

"Good night, Pritchard," he said, and because he felt happy and good he put his arm round her waist and kissed her on the lips.

Her lips were very soft. They lingered on his, and she returned his kiss. It was the warm, hearty embrace of a healthy woman in the prime of life. He found it very pleasant, and he held her to him a little more closely. She put her arms round his neck.

As a general rule he did not wake till Pritchard came in with his letters, but next morning he woke at half past seven. He had a curious sensation that he did not recognize. He was accustomed to sleep with two pillows under his head, and he suddenly grew aware of the fact that he had only one. Then he remembered and with a start looked round. The other pillow was beside his own. Thank

God, no sleeping head rested there, but it was plain that one had. His heart sank. He broke out into a cold sweat.

"My God, what a fool I've been!" he cried out loud.

How could he have done anything so stupid? What on earth had come over him? He was the last man to play about with servant girls. What a disgraceful thing to do! At his age and in his position. He had not heard Pritchard slip away. He must have been asleep. It wasn't even as if he'd liked her very much. She wasn't his type. And as he had said the other night, she rather bored him. Even now he only knew her as Pritchard. He had no notion what her first name was. What madness! And what was to happen now? The position was impossible. It was obvious he couldn't keep her, and yet to send her away for what was his fault as much as hers seemed shockingly unfair. How idiotic to lose the best parlormaid a man ever had just for an hour's folly!

He needn't have worried, Maugham tells us on the final page.

She *was* a perfect treasure and their lives would resume as before.

Maugham once said: "There are three rules for writing well; unfortunately, no one knows what they are." He might have added "and that goes for sex scenes as well."

Sex is at the core of nearly all Maugham's stories and novels, but it always occurs off camera. The closest thing to a description of seduction occurs in his 1915 masterpiece *Of Human Bondage*.

Philip Carey is a young London medical student who falls desperately in love with Mildred Rogers, a pretty but slutty waitress. She treats him miserably, but he can't help himself: "He hated her, he despised her, he loved her with all his heart."

Philip limps from a congenital club foot which Mildred doesn't let him forget.

She has walked out on him several times and finally hits bottom, becoming a streetwalker—but he still takes her back into his apartment. She has never slept with him, but now she is desperate and needs him, so she is determined to wheedle her way back into his affections.

"Can I sit down?" she said.

Before he could answer, she settled herself on his knees.

"If you're not going to bed, you'd better go and put on a dressing gown."

"Oh, I'm all right as I am." Then putting her arms round his neck, she placed her face against his and said: "Why are you so horrid to me, Phil?"

He tried to get up, but she would not let him.

"I do love you, Philip," she said.

"Don't talk damned rot."

"It isn't, it's true. I can't live without you. I want you."

He released himself from her arms.

"Please get up. You're making a fool of yourself and you're making me feel a perfect idiot."

"I love you, Philip. I want to make up for all the harm I did you. I can't go on like this; it's not in human nature."

He slipped out of the chair and left her in it.

"I'm very sorry, but it's too late." She gave a heartrending sob.

"But why? How can you be so cruel?"

"I suppose it's because I loved you too much. I wore the passion out. The thought of anything of that sort horrifies me. I can't look at you now without thinking of Emil and Griffiths. One can't help those things; I suppose it's just nerves."

She seized his hand and covered it with kisses.

"Don't," he cried.

She sank back into the chair.

"I can't go on like this. If you won't love me, I'd rather go away."

"Don't be foolish, you haven't anywhere to go. You can stay here as long as you like, but it must be on the definite understanding that we're friends and nothing more." Then she dropped suddenly the vehemence of passion and gave a soft, insinuating laugh. She sidled up to Philip and put her arms round him. She made her voice low and wheedling.

"Don't be such an old silly. I believe you're nervous. You don't know how nice I can be."

She put her face against his and rubbed his cheek with hers. To Philip, her smile was an abominable leer, and the suggestive glitter of her eyes filled him with horror. He drew back instinctively.

"I won't," he said.

But she would not let him go. She sought his mouth with her lips. He took her hands and tore them roughly apart and pushed her away.

"You disgust me," he said.

"Me?"

She steadied herself with one hand on the chimney-piece. She looked at him for an instant, and two red spots suddenly appeared on her cheeks. She gave a shrill, angry laugh.

"I disgust *you*."

She paused and drew in her breath sharply. Then she burst into a furious torrent of abuse. She shouted at the top of her voice. She called him every foul name she could think of. She used language so obscene that Philip was astounded; she was always so anxious to be refined, so shocked by coarseness, that it had never occurred to him that she knew the words she used now. She came up to him and thrust her face in his. It was distorted with passion, and in her tumultuous speech the spittle dribbled over her lips.

"I never cared for you, not once, I was making a fool of you always, you bored me, you bored me stiff, and I hated you, I would never have let you touch me only for the money, and it used to make me sick when I had to let you kiss me. We laughed at you, Griffiths and me; we laughed because you was such a mug. A mug! A mug!"

Then she burst again into abominable invective. She accused him of every mean fault; she said he was stingy, she said he was dull, she said he was vain selfish; she cast virulent ridicule on everything upon which he was most sensitive. And at last she turned to go. She kept on, with hysterical violence, shouting at him an opprobrious, filthy epithet. She seized the hand of the door and flung it open. Then she turned round and hurled at him the injury which she knew was the only one that really touched him. She threw into the word all the malice and all the venom of which she was capable. She flung it at him as though it were a blow.

"Cripple!"

The scene in the marvelous 1934 film follows the one in the novel almost exactly, except that Bette Davis, or the director, or the writer embellished the diatribe by adding this venomous cockney line:

> MILDRED: And, when you kissed me, I woiped moy mouth, (demonstrates, wiping lips with back of hand) woiped moy mouth!

Few authors have written about sexual relationships between men and women as well as Maugham, yet ironically, his heart, or hormones, were not truly in it. For example, Sinclair Lewis told me that "the Mildred [in] *Of Human Bondage* was, in real life, a *male* waiter."

Not long after his one disastrous marriage dissolved, Maugham wrote in an article (suppressed later by her family):

> "I always considered myself to be one-third queer and two-thirds straight. It would appear it was actually the other way around."

In a well-known showbiz anecdote, Maugham, after a late dinner with producer Garson Kanin and his wife, Ruth Gordon, said:

"Well, it's late, and I'd best be getting to bed if I'm to keep my youth."

"Why Willie," exclaimed Ms. Gordon, "you should have brought him!"

3

Tame But Good

Life's three greatest things:
the Martini before and the cigarette after.
Anon

J OYCE C AROL O ATES HAS WRITTEN MANY FINE NOVELS AND SHORT stories. She isn't always so lady like as she is in the following charming vignette, called "Old Budapest."

She heard laughter from the other room. She was ready to return with her various lemon slices when someone entered the kitchen behind her. She heard the floorboards gently creaking; but no one spoke. It might be Tommy playfully tiptoeing up behind her...it might be the deputy chief of mission come to see what was taking her so long...it might be the cultural attaché on an errand, sent to fetch more Brazil nuts (the men had been eating them rather gluttonously) or cocktail napkins. Marianne didn't turn but she saw a tall ghostly reflection in an aluminum door to one of the cupboards: tall: which (fortunately) ruled out the director of public relations who was hardly more than her height. She couldn't identify the man but she chose not to turn in surprise; instead she pretended to be cutting a final lemon slice, nervously aware of her pretty small-boned hands....

He gripped her shoulder; Marianne instinctively closed her eyes, and rested her head back against him as they kissed; and immediately she felt a splendid rush of emotion, hazy, sweet, familiar, she was sixteen years old, she was fourteen, even thirteen, being kissed in a doorway...being kissed surreptitiously at a party...breathless in a corner, her heart beating hard, her eyes shut...She might have been even younger, ten or eleven, practicing kisses against the mirror in her bedroom, secret and daring.

It was a gentle kiss, experimental, improvised. Marianne responded with a small frisson of surprise, a semblance of surprise. She was touching his arm lightly, she hoped she had wiped off the lemon juice, how sweet to be approached with such tact and delicacy, in so gentlemanly a fashion, she thought suddenly of the Hungarian editor and herself walking on Gellert Hill, and along the Danube, the warm moist sunshine heavy with the smell of lilacs, so many romantic couples, lovers, the young ones amorous as puppies, but there were middle-aged lovers too, Marianne was embarrassed to see a man and a woman in their fifties, pressed close together on a stone bench, kissing with such frank and impassioned energy that they must have been oblivious of their surroundings... and Otto said in an undertone, "Romance is desperation and we are a desperate people—we laugh a great deal too."

Now she felt the kiss deepen, and a feathery-light sensation ran through her body, her belly, her loins, a sensation familiar enough but always in a way new, and reassuring, and impersonal; and in another second or two the tenor of the kiss would change and become more serious: the man would part her lips, his tongue would prod at hers, his teeth grind lightly against hers, they would still be smiling but the kiss would have become serious, and Marianne's plans for the rest of the day—was this Saturday?—might have to be substantially altered.

This small, subtle, anecdotal piece is worth reading in its entirety. A lot of clues to Marianne's back story and character are sneaked into just a few words by a fine writer.

Ernest Hemingway was known mostly for the doings of macho men in macho situations, but, of course, he did write about men and women and love and sex in many of his novels and stories. But even the famous sleeping bag scene in his 1940 novel *For Whom the Bell Tolls*, which was the talk of reading America at the time, while pretty graphic for Hemingway, was not exactly Jackie Collins. Here's some background and a bit of the bag scene:

Robert Jordan, a young American fighting against the Fascists in the Spanish Civil War, is camped in the hills with his fellow guerilla group. A beautiful young girl, Maria, is rescued from the enemy. She is very innocent, but she is enamored of Jordan, and one night she steals into his sleeping bag. He has a pistol next to him and she feels it, but he is quick to laugh and reassure her that it is just a gun (which can't fail to remind a reader of Mae West's famous quip, "Is that a gun in your pocket or are you just glad to see me?").

After some stilted preliminary talk comes some more stilted talk:

> "I love thee, Maria," he said. "And no one has done anything to thee. Thee, they cannot touch. No one has touched thee, little rabbit."
>
> "You believe that?"
>
> "I know it."
>
> "And you can love me?" warm again against him now.
>
> "I can love thee more."
>
> "I will try to kiss thee very well."
>
> "Kiss me a little."
>
> "I do not know how."
>
> "Just kiss me."
>
> She kissed him on the cheek.
>
> "No."
>
> "Where do the noses go? I always wondered where the noses would go."

(It is a silly scene and not very sexy, but all over America couples were soon parodying: "Where do the noses go?" before they kissed.)

A few moments later in the sleeping bag comes this dialogue:

> "...Am I thy woman now?"
>
> "Yes, Maria. Yes, my little rabbit."
>
> She held herself tight to him and her lips looked for his and then found them and were against them and he felt her, fresh, new and smooth and young and lovely with the warm, scalding

coolness and unbelievable to be there in the robe that was as familiar as his clothes, or his shoes, or his duty and then she said,
frightenedly, "And now let us do quickly what it is we do so that
the other is all gone."

"You want?"

"Yes," she said almost fiercely. "Yes. Yes. Yes."

The scene ends there, and that's all the reader is going to get. In a
later sexual encounter with Maria, Jordan waxes orgasmic:

"Well, then. Oh, then. Oh, then. Oh."

Then there was the smell of heather crushed and the rough-
ness of the bent stalks under her head and the sun bright on her
closed eyes and all his life he would remember the curve of her
throat with her head pushed back into the heather roots and her
lips that moved smally and by themselves and the fluttering of the
lashes on the eyes tight closed against the sun and against everything, and for her everything was red, orange, gold-red from the
sun on the closed eyes, and it all was that color, all of it, the filling,
the possessing, the having, all of that color, all in a blindness of
that color. For him it was a dark passage which led to nowhere,
then to nowhere, then again to nowhere, once again to nowhere,
always and forever to nowhere, heavy on the elbows in the earth
to nowhere, dark, never any end to nowhere, hung on all time
always to unknowing nowhere, this time and again for always to
nowhere, now not to be borne once again always and to nowhere,
now beyond all bearing up, up, up and into nowhere, suddenly,
scaldingly, holdingly all nowhere gone and time absolutely still and
they were both there, time having stopped and he felt the earth
move out and away from under them.

Then he was lying on his side, his head deep in the heather,
smelling it and the smell of the roots and the earth and the sun
came through it and it was scratchy on his bare shoulders and
along his flanks and the girl was lying opposite him with her eyes
still shut and then she opened them and smiled at him and he said
very tiredly and from a great but friendly distance, "Hello, rabbit."

Then Maria says:

"Thou hast loved many others."
"Some. But not as thee."
"And it was not thus? Truly?"
"It was a pleasure but it was not thus."
"And then the earth moved. The earth never moved before?"
"Nay. Truly never."

Thus did the earth-moving phrase enter the American idiom. All over the country, couples were asking each other's "little rabbit" if the earth had moved after making love.

Author Stella Hyde, with tongue firmly in cheek, praises Hemingway for "making the first literary link between human sexual activity and tectonic plate shifting."

In an early Ray Bradbury story, "The Best of All Possible Worlds," the author wrote this line:

"The first six months of our marriage, the earth did not move, it shook."

Parodies of Hemingway's novel and its prose style sprang up everywhere. One in the *New Yorker* magazine by Cornelia Otis Skinner entitled "For Whom the Gong Bongs," had such lines as this:

"Hast thou yet blown up the streetcar, Ingles?"
"Obscenity, obscenity, obscenity," he replied, not unkindly.

The great writer Vladimir Nabokov did not admire Hemingway, commenting:

"I read him for the first time in the early forties, something about bells, balls, and bulls, and loathed it."

For Whom the Bell Tolls was an enormously successful novel (and film) and, though considered rather daring in its sex scenes, it encountered no censorship. In the twenties, Hemingway had written a story called

"Up In Michigan" about a youthful seduction that Hemingway wanted to include in his group of stories *In Our Time*, but Max Perkins, his editor at Scribners, cut it out. The author tried again to include it in his next book of short stories, *Men Without Women*.

As he often did, Perkins asked Scott Fitzgerald for his advice. Scott admitted that "one line *at least* was pornographic," but he added, "what good was a story about a seduction without the seduction?"

Hemingway *did not* attempt to insert the story in another collection of stories. (It can now be found in *The Complete Short Stories of Ernest Hemingway*, Scribners, 1987).

Here is the scene Perkins found offensive:

> They sat down in the shelter of the warehouse and Jim pulled Liz close to him. She was frightened. One of Jim's hands went inside her dress and stroked over her breast and the other hand was in her lap. She was very frightened and didn't know how he was going to go about things but she snuggled close to him. Then the hand that felt so big in her lap went away and was on her leg and started to move up it.
>
> "Don't, Jim," Liz said. Jim slid the hand further up.
>
> "You mustn't, Jim. You mustn't." Neither Jim nor Jim's big hand paid any attention to her.
>
> The boards were hard. Jim had her dress up and was trying to do something to her. She was frightened but she wanted it. She had to have it but it frightened her.
>
> "You mustn't do it, Jim. You mustn't."
>
> "I got to. I'm going to. You know we got to."
>
> "No we haven't, Jim. We ain't got to. Oh, it isn't right. Oh, it's so big and it hurts so. You can't. Oh, Jim. Jim. Oh."
>
> The hemlock planks of the dock were hard and splintery and cold and Jim was heavy on her and he had hurt her. Liz pushed him, she was so uncomfortable and cramped. Jim was asleep. He wouldn't move.

It's not too difficult to figure out which line Fitzgerald was referring to. So this scene is not particularly sexy, but in Perkins' reaction to it we see the puritanical side of publishing in the America of the era.

_4_

"What Is This Thing Called, Love?":
The First Time[1]

READERS HAVE ALWAYS BEEN INTERESTED IN "THE FIRST TIME," whether for the girl or the boy or both. It doesn't have to be a detailed account of the actual act; it can be merely a description of the first sexual arousal.

People tend to think of _Gone With the Wind_ as a sexy book. They are probably thinking of the film, particularly the scene where Rhett sweeps a coy Scarlett into his manly arms and carries her up the big staircase to a bedroom as the music soars. The scene is not in the book.

Here is the scene in Margaret Mitchell's novel where Scarlett, though having been already married twice, finally feels true sexuality for the first time—in spite of herself.

The scene takes place just after the funeral of Scarlett's second husband. Rhett has just casually asked her to marry him, and she has asserted that she will never marry again.

> "Nonsense. Why?"
> "I said you'd had bad luck and what you've just said proves it. You've been married to a boy and to an old man. And into the bargain I'll bet your mother told you that women must bear 'these things' because of the compensating joys of motherhood. Well,

---

[1] The title of this chapter illustrates the surprising power of a simple comma—as shown even better in Peter De Vries' parody of _Moby Dick_: "Call me, Ishmael—feel free to call me anytime."

that's all wrong. Why not try marrying a fine young man who has a bad reputation and a way with women? It'll be fun."

"You are coarse and conceited and I think this conversation has gone far enough. It's—it's quite vulgar."

"And quite enjoyable too, isn't it? I'll wager you never discussed the marital relation with a man before, even Charles or Frank."

She scowled at him. Rhett knew too much. She wondered where he had learned all he knew about women. It wasn't decent.

"Rhett, do be sensible. I don't want to marry anybody."

"Scarlett O'Hara, you're a fool!"

Before she could withdraw her mind from its far places, his arms were around her, as sure and hard as on the dark road to Tara, so long ago. She felt again the rush of helplessness, the sinking yielding, the surging tide of warmth that left her limp. And the quiet face of Ashley Wilkes was blurred and drowned to nothingness. He bent back her head across his arm and kissed her, softly at first, and then with a swift gradation of intensity that made her cling to him as the only solid thing in a dizzy swaying world. His insistent mouth was parting her shaking lips, sending wild tremors along her nerves, evoking from her sensations she had never known she was capable of feeling. And before a swimming giddiness spun her round and round, she knew that she was kissing him back.

"Stop—please, I'm faint!" she whispered, trying to turn her head weakly from him. He pressed her head back hard against his shoulder and she had a dizzy glimpse of his face. His eyes were wide and blazing queerly and the tremor in his arms frightened her.

"I want to make you faint. I will make you faint. You've had this coming to you for years. None of the fools you've known have kissed you like this—have they? Your precious Charles or Frank or your stupid Ashley—"

"Please—"

"I said your stupid Ashley. Gentlemen all—what do they know about women? What did they know about you? I know you."

His mouth was on hers again and she surrendered without a struggle, too weak even to turn her head, without even the desire to turn it, her heart shaking her with its poundings, fear of his strength and her nerveless weakness sweeping her. What was he going to do? She would faint if he did not stop. If he would only stop—if he would never stop.

"Say Yes!" His mouth was poised above hers and his eyes were so close that they seemed enormous, filling the world. "Say Yes, damn you, or—"

She whispered "Yes" before she even thought. It was almost as if he had willed the word and she had spoken it without her own volition.

Now would be a good time for Rhett to sweep her into his arms and mount the staircase to the bedroom—but, no,—Rhett leaves for London, returns with a huge diamond ring, and they are married. (Not happily, ultimately).

Anäis Nin was renowned for her tasteful, erotic scenes (and perhaps more for her longtime romance with Henry Miller). During the 1940s, she and Miller wrote porno for a "collector" for a dollar a page at a time when they were broke in Paris. They hadn't expected to publish these pieces, but in 1969 the writings were published as *Delta of Venus*. The following is a small anecdotal sketch of a virginal encounter included in the book:

One evening some years ago, a fisherman's daughter of eighteen was walking along the edge of the sea, leaping from rock to rock, her white dress clinging to her body. Walking thus and dreaming and watching the effects of the moon on the sea, the soft lapping of the waves at her feet, she came to a hidden cove where she noticed that someone was swimming. She could see only the head moving and occasionally an arm. The swimmer was quite far away. Then she heard a light voice calling out to her, "Come in and swim. It's beautiful." It was said in Spanish with a foreign accent. "Hello, Maria," it called, so the voice knew her. It must have been one of the young American women who bathed there during the day.

She answered, "Who are you?"

"I'm Evelyn," said the voice, "come and swim with me!"

It was very tempting. Maria could easily take off her white dress and wear only her short white chemise. She looked everywhere. There was no one around. The sea was calm and speckled with moonlight. For the first time Maria understood the European love of midnight bathing. She took off her dress. She had long black hair, a pale face, slanted green eyes, greener than the sea. She was beautifully formed, with high breasts, long legs, a stylized body. She knew how to swim better than any other woman on the island. She slid into the water and began her long easy strokes towards Evelyn.

Evelyn swam under the water, came up to her and gripped her legs. In the water they teased each other. The semidarkness and the bathing cap made it difficult to see the face clearly. American women had voices like boys.

Evelyn wrestled with Maria, embraced her under the water. They came up for air, laughing, swimming nonchalantly away and back to each other. Maria's chemise floated up around her shoulders and hampered her movements. Finally it came off altogether and she was left naked. Evelyn swam under and touched her playfully, wrestling and diving under and between her legs.

Evelyn would part her legs so that her friend could dive between them and reappear on the other side. She floated and let her friend swim under her arched back.

Maria saw that she was naked too. Then suddenly she felt Evelyn embracing her from behind, covering her whole body with hers. The water was lukewarm, like a luxuriant pillow, so salty that it bore them, helped them to float and swim without effort.

"You're beautiful, Maria," said the deep voice, and Evelyn kept her arms around her. Maria wanted to float away, but she was held by the warmth of the water, the constant touch of her friend's body. She let herself be embraced. She did not feel breasts on her friend, but, then, she knew young American women she had seen did not have breasts. Maria's body was languid, and she wanted to close her eyes.

Suddenly what she felt between her legs was not a hand but something else, something so unexpected, so disturbing that she screamed. This was no Evelyn but a young man, Evelyn's younger brother, and he had slipped his erect penis between her legs. She screamed but no one heard, and her scream was only something she had been trained to expect of herself. In reality his embrace seemed to her as lulling and warming and caressing as the water. The water and the penis and the hands conspired to arouse her body.

She tried to swim away. But the boy swam under her body, caressed her, gripped her legs, and then mounted her again from behind.

In the water they wrestled, but each movement affected her only more physically, made her more aware of his body against hers, of his hands upon her. The water swung her breasts back and forth like two heavy water lilies floating. He kissed them. With the constant motion he could not really take her, but his penis touched her over and over again in the most vulnerable tip of her sex, and Maria was losing her strength. She swam towards shore, and he followed. They fell on the sand. The waves still lapped them as they lay there panting, naked. The boy then took the girl, and the sea came and washed over them and washed away the virgin blood.

From that night they met only at this hour. He took her there in the water, swaying, floating. The wavelike movements of their bodies as they enjoyed each other seemed part of the sea. They found a foothold on a rock and stood together, caressed by the waves, and shaking from the orgasm.

When I went down to the beach at night, I often felt as though I could see them, swimming together, making love.

In terms of sex, the first time can mean many things. In Ethan Canin's 1988 novel, *The Year of Getting to Know Us*, the first time is the shock of a sixteen-year-old boy's learning about his father's extracurricular sex life in a bizarre way. The father goes out a lot in his beloved Lincoln but doesn't take his son, who wants to be closer to his father. His mother urges him to go sometime with his father even if he has "to sneak along," which he does one afternoon, hiding in the trunk of his father's car.

On the freeway the thermal seams whizzed and popped in my ears. The ride had smoothed out now, as the shocks settled into the high speed, hardly dipping on curves, muffling everything as if we were under water. As far as I could tell, we were still driving west, toward the ocean. I sat halfway up and rested my back against the golf bag. I could see shapes now inside the trunk. When we slowed down and the blinker went on, I attempted bearings, but the sun was the same in all directions and the trunk lid was without shadow. We braked hard. I felt the car leave the freeway. We made turns. We went straight. Then more turns, and as we slowed down and I was stretching out, uncurling my body along the diagonal, we made a sharp right onto gravel and pulled over and stopped.

My father opened the door. The car dipped and rocked, shuddered. The engine clicked. Then the passenger door opened. I waited.

If I heard her voice today, twenty-six years later, I would recognize it.

"Angel," she said.

I heard the weight of their bodies sliding across the back seat, first hers, then his. They weren't three feet away. I curled up, crouched into the low space between the golf bag and the back of the passenger compartment. There were two firm points in the cushion where it was displaced. As I lay there, I went over the voice again in my head: it was nobody I knew. I heard a laugh from her, and then something low from him. I felt the shift of the trunk's false rear, and then, as I lay behind them, I heard the contact: the crinkle of clothing, arms wrapping, and the half-delicate, muscular sounds. It was like hearing a television in the next room. His voice once more, and then the rising of their breath, slow; a minute of this, maybe another; then shifting again, the friction of cloth on the leather seat and the car's soft rocking. "Dad," I whispered. Then rocking again; my father's sudden panting, harder and harder, his half-words. The car shook violently. "Dad," I whispered. I shouted, "Dad!"

The door opened.

His steps kicked up gravel. I heard jingling metal, the sound of the key in the trunk lock. He was standing over me in an explosion of light.

He said, "Put back the club socks."

I did and got out of the car to stand next to him. He rubbed his hands down the front of his shirt.

"What the hell," he said.

"I was in the trunk."

"I know," he said. "What the goddamn."

This is not just a dirty anecdote, like almost good sex writing, but here we learn a great deal about the character of the boy, the father, and even the long-suffering mother.

And, we don't really *have* to see what they did in the back seat, do we? We know—*they did plenty.*

We find a similar situation, but a less plot-altering episode, in John Cheever's best seller of 1954, *The Wapshot Chronicles*. Young Moses is trying to rescue Rosalie from a minor boating misadventure.

> Then he let the motor idle and began to shout: "Rosalie, Rosalie, Rosalie, Rosalie..."
>
> She answered him in a little while, and he saw the outlines of the *Tern* and told her what line to throw him, and lifted her, in his arms, off the bow. She was laughing, and he had been so anxious that her cheerfulness seemed to him like a kind of goodness that he had not suspected her to have. Then they picked up the skiff and headed for shore and when the *Tern* was moored they went into the old clubhouse that looked as if it had been put together by old ladies and mice and had, in fact, been floated down the river from St. Botolphs. Moses built a fire and they dried themselves here and would have remained if old Mr. Sturgis hadn't come into the billiard room to practice shots.
>
> Honora finished her hooked rug that afternoon—a field of red roses—and this and the gloomy sea-turn decided her to go to West Farm at last and be introduced to the stranger. She cut across the fields in the rain from Boat Street to River Street and let herself in the side door calling, "Hello. Hello. Is anyone home?" There was no answer. The house was empty. She was not nosy, but she climbed the stairs to the spare room to see if the girl might be there. The hastily made bed, the clothes scattered on chairs, and the full ash tray made her feel unfriendly and suspicious and she opened the closet door. She was in the closet when she heard Moses and Rosalie coming up the stairs, Moses saying, "What harm can there be in something that would make us both feel so good?" Honora closed the closet door as they came into the room.

What else Honora heard—and she heard plenty—does not concern us here. This is not a clinical account. We will only consider the dilemma of an old lady, born in Polynesia, educated at Miss Wilbur's, a philanthropist and Samaritan, led by no more than her search for the truth into a narrow closet on a rainy afternoon. *She heard plenty.*

Once again the reader is asked to furnish the details in his or her own mind. It is a good device and an old, oft-used one.

People did not—and do not—read one of America's most internationally famous writers, Sinclair Lewis, awarded America's first Nobel Prize for Literature (1930), for sexual scenes. And they are therefore seldom disappointed in such perennial classics as *Main Street*, *Elmer Gantry*, *Bobbitt*, and *Arrowsmith*. These novels all contain men and women, some romance and marriage. But sex? It is interesting for the modern-day writer, who is free to say and describe virtually anything in the bedroom, to see how gingerly sex was handled half a century ago.

The following, from Lewis's 1945 novel, *Cass Timberlane*, is as close as he gets to a sex scene:

> Judge Timberlane has just married the much younger Jinny Marshland, and they are aboard a train on their honeymoon. They have different berths; I guess this is because berths were small and not very private. Jinny visits the judge during the night and says:
>
> "Of course you would never even hint at it, but I do imagine you'd like to know, so now I can tell you—and I'm darned if I know whether this is a boast or a confession—but if it interests you, I'm still a virgin."
>
> Suddenly he grew up a little, and he was placid in saying, "Yes, it does interest me, and I'm glad, though I don't think I'd've been ugly if it had been the opposite. And I love you madly and you go back to bed or I'll spank hell out of you."
>
> "Right here in public? In my pajamas? I dare you to!" she said, and kissed him and was gone.

The next day Jinny and Cass go to a fancy resort in Florida and things heat up a bit. But...

> They shut the door against a world of intrusive friendliness. They faced each other, and he understood her shyness and tried to speak as he thought her Gang at Miss Hatter's would speak:

"Well, baby, this is it. I guess we're up against it. But let me explain that I'm not just violently in love with you. I'm also extremely fond of you."

She was shivering, but she tried to be merry.

"They all make so much of this accidental virtue of virginity that you get scared about it, and the wedding night—I suppose this is our real wedding-night—is a combination of getting drunk and winning a million-dollar lottery and waiting to be hanged. Animals are a lot wiser."

He was tense with listening, and Jinny, in his arms, was as impersonal to him as a pillow, and apprehensively he realized that he could no more make ardent love to her now than to that pillow.

Was he going to be a failure as lover with this one girl whom he had loved utterly?

She muttered, with almost prayerful earnestness, "Was the bathroom the third door on the right or the second? I'd hate to go rocketing in on some old maid!"

He laughed then, and lost his apprehensiveness. But as he kissed her it was she who had become fearful and unyielding, and in pity for her his ardor sank to a gentle stroking of her cheek.

When she seemed to have relaxed a little, to be expectant, his intensity had so worn him that he could only hold her softly, while fear crept through him again, and he stammered, "I've heard of such things but I never expected—I find I'm so fond of you, and maybe scared of you, that just now I can't even make love to you."

She answered as sweetly and briskly as though they were discussing a picnic-basket.

"Yes, I've heard of it. Temporary—not matter a bit. Oh, you'd be surprised at all the things Lyra and Wilma and I used to talk about. Don't worry. I love just lying with my cheek on your shoulder—now that I've found a comparatively regular valley among the jagged peaks of your shoulder blades. Dear darling!"

They were almost instantly asleep and Cass came to life at dawn to sit up and see, on her own side of the bed, curled like a cat and rosily sleeping, his adored and inviolate bride.

On the third day, they move to a rustic cabin on the beach, and matters get much better. They have some Daiquiris and—things happen:

There were no occupied shacks near them, no whispering lady guests, but only the sliding sea. They lay with the door half open to the night, and suddenly he was ruthless with love and she as fierce as he, nipping his ear with angry little teeth, and they fell asleep in the surprise of love.

At dawn, Cass woke her and they ran down the beach and bathed, unclad and laughing, and came back to new abandonment.

Jinny marveled, "We both seem to be great successes. It was a terrible shock at first, but now I do cleave to you and we are one flesh."

"Forever?"

"Forever and ever, beloved!"

Sleeping and waking, waking and sleeping, their open door embracing the wash of the fertile tide, amazed by the curiousness of arms and legs and breasts, redeemed from civilization they lay about the tousled bed till noon...

And that's it. Pretty tame. It was written all the way back in 1945, and it was pretty racy then for a mainstream novel. And, it was written by one of the best-selling authors of all time. Not sexy, but it is important to see the chasm between then and now in the sex writing department.

However, in 1956, things got racier. Readers could talk of little else but Grace Metalious and her small-town novel, *Peyton Place*. Here is our heroine's first sexual encounter:

He went to her quickly and raised her to her feet with his hands under her elbows. In the second before he kissed her, she had thought fleetingly that she was glad she had remembered to wear flat-heeled shoes. In flat heels, the top of her head came exactly to Brad's eyebrows.

He raised his lips but did not take his arms from around her. "Almost, but not quite," he said softly.

"What?"

"Almost but not quite a woman," he said. "You kiss like a child."

In the firelight she could see her reflection in his eyes. "How do you do that?" she asked, her breath hurting in her chest.

"What?"

"Kiss like a woman?"

"Open your mouth a little," he said, and kissed her again...

Brad was practiced and polished, an expert who regarded the making of love as a creative art. He had led her well through the preliminaries of sex, undressing her deftly and quickly.

"Don't," he said, when she turned her face away from him and closed her eyes. He put his fingers to her cheek and brought her face back toward his own. "If you are going to feel shame, Allison, it is not going to be any good for you, not tonight or any other night. Tell me what it is that makes you turn away from me, and I'll take care of it or explain it away. But don't begin by closing your eyes so that you don't have to look at me."

"I've never been naked in front of anyone before," she said, against his shoulder.

"Don't use that word 'naked'," he said. "There is a world of difference in referring to yourself as nude. Nude is a word as smooth as your hips," he said, caressing her, "but naked has the sound of a rock being turned over to expose maggots. Now, what is it about being nude that embarrasses you?"

She hesitated..."I'm afraid that you'll find me ugly," she said at last.

"I am not going to say anything, because no matter what reassurances I made in this moment, every one would sound false to you. Besides, that is not what you are afraid of, you know."

"What is it then?"

"You are afraid that I will think badly of you for allowing me to have you. It is a perfectly normal feminine fear. If I gave you a reason that was convincing enough for why you are doing as you are, this fear would leave you. It is an odd thing, but most women need excuses of one kind or another. It is much easier for men."

"How?" she had smiled at his descriptions of women.

"A man says, 'Ah, here is a gorgeous creature whom I should love to take to bed.' Then he begins to work toward his goal. If he achieves it, he jumps into the nearest bed with her and fornicates for all he is worth, before she can change her mind and demand that he present her with a good reason for what she is doing."

She turned onto her back and put her arms over her head. "Then you think that sex between unmarried persons is excusable."

"I've never thought of it as being either excusable or inexcusable. It is just there, and it can be good if people just won't mess it up with reasons and apologies. Have you understood one word I've said?"

"Yes, I think so."

"May I look at you, then?"

She had clenched her fists, but she did not close her eyes or turn away from him. "Yes," she said.

He did it slowly, following with his eyes the path created by his hands as they traveled over her.

"You are truly beautiful," he said. "You have the long, aristocratic legs and the exquisite breasts of a statue."

She let out her long-held breath with a sigh that made her quiver, and her heart beat hard under her breasts. He placed his lips against the pulsating spot, while he pressed gently at her abdomen with his hand. He continued to kiss her and stroke her until her whole body trembled under his lips and hands. When he kissed the softness of her inner thighs, she began to make moaning, animal sounds, and even then he continued his sensual touching and stroking and waited until she began the undulating movements of intercourse with her hips. She was lying with her arms bent and raised over her head, and he held her pinned to the bed with his hands on her wrists.

"Don't," he commanded, when she tried to twist away from him at the first thrust of pain. "Help me," he said. "Don't pull away."

"I can't," she cried. "I can't."

"Yes, you can. Press your heels against the mattress and raise your hips. Help me. Quickly!"

In the last moment a bright drop of blood appeared on her mouth, where she had bitten into her lips, and then she had cried out the odd, mingled cry of pain and pleasure.

Later, after they had smoked and talked, he turned to her again.

"It is never as good as it should be for a woman, the first time," he said. "This one will be for you."

He began to woo her again, with words, and kisses, and touches, and this time she had felt the full, soaring joy of pleasure without pain.

"I thought I was dying," she said to him, afterward. "And it was the loveliest feeling in the world."

By Sunday morning, she had been able to walk nude in front of Brad, and feel his eyes probing her, without feeling either shame or fear. She had arched her back, and lifted her heavy hair off her neck, and pressed her breasts against his face, and gloried in his swift reaction to her.

This is what it is like she had thought exultantly, to be in love with a man with everything that is within oneself.

Too soon, it was Sunday night, and they made their way back to New York over the Merritt Parkway. Brad held her fingers in his and she giggled.

"It would be terrible if I got pregnant," she had said, thinking that it would not be terrible at all, "because then we'd have to get married and I'd never get any work done. We'd be spending all our time in bed."

Brad withdrew his hand from hers at once.

"But my dear child," he said, "I was extremely conscientious about taking precautions against anything as disastrous as pregnancy. I am already married. I thought you knew."

She had felt nothing but a numbness which seemed to insulate her body with ice.

"No," she said, in a conversational tone, "I didn't know. Do you and your wife have children?"

"Two," said Brad.

She should have felt something, but the nothingness inside her would not dislodge itself.

"I see," she said.

"I'm surprised that you didn't know. Everyone does. David Noyes knows it. He met my wife in the office one day, as a matter of fact."

"He never mentioned it to me," she said as if she were talking about someone who had met a vague acquaintance and had attached no importance to it.

"Well," said Brad, with a little laugh, "Bernice is not the type who impresses a stranger on a first meeting."

But what about a book that was written many years before and shook the writing of sex in the English language forever?

5

A Watershed in Sexual Literature

I am one, Sir, that comes to tell you your daughter and
the Moor are now making the beast with two backs.
Shakespeare

ONE DAY, OUR CLEANING LADY, VIOLA (PRONOUNCED VI-*OH*-LAH)
saw a copy of *Lady Chatterly's Lover* on my desk and asked if she could
read it. The next day it was returned with this note:

> "Thank you for lending me the book. Mrs. Chatterly didn't
> know what she *wanted* but she sure knew what she *needed!*"

That was very likely the best pithy review of the book ever.

In 1928, D. (David) H. (Herbert) Lawrence wrote the novel and
published it privately himself in France. Declared obscene, it was banned,
and it became a sensational underground blockbuster. The book could
not be obtained on the open market until 1960, when its literary merit
was seen to justify its astonishing candor about sexual matters. What is
often overlooked is that in and around the book's explicit sexual scenes
lies a fine depiction of the strictly defined levels of British society which
persisted even after World War I.

"It's more about class than ass," a literary friend of mine lyrically
opined.

I believe it is a pivotal and well-written book that was much maligned
and herein deserves a long excerpt.

Certainly the main thrust of the novel is not about game manage-
ment, though Oliver Mellors, the eponymous protagonist, meets his
boss's wife over an issue concerning some pheasants he was raising on
the boss's estate.

Connie Chatterly is a lovely, lonely young woman who is married
to cold, impotent Sir Clifford who has come back from the war crippled
and bitter. Connie is depressed at being childless, lonely, and emotional.
She comes across some baby pheasants near the gamekeeper's modest
cottage at the end of the estate. Mellors is actually an intelligent and
educated man who pretends to be a simple peasant. The following relates
their first real encounter:

He turned again to look at her. She was kneeling and holding
her two hands slowly forward, blindly, so that the chicken should
run in to the mother hen again. And there was something so mute
and forlorn in her, compassion flamed in his bowels for her.

Without knowing, he came quickly towards her and crouched
beside her again, taking the chick from her hands, because she was
afraid of the hen, and putting it back in the coop. At the back of
his loins the fire suddenly darted stronger.

He glanced apprehensively at her. Her face was averted,
and she was crying blindly, in all the anguish of her generation's
forlornness. His heart melted suddenly, like a drop of fire, and he
put out his hand and laid his fingers on her knee.

"You shouldn't cry," he said softly.

But then she put her hands over her face and felt that really
her heart was broken and nothing mattered any more.

He laid his hand on her shoulder, and softly, gently, it began
to travel down the curve of her back, blindly, with a blind stroking
motion, to the curve of her crouching loins. And there his hand
softly, softly, stroked the curve of her flank, in the blind instinc-
tive caress.

She had found her scrap of handkerchief and was blindly
trying to dry her face.

"Shall you come to the hut?" he said, in a quiet, neutral voice.

And closing his hand softly on her upper arm, he drew her
up and led her slowly to the hut, not letting go of her till she was
inside. Then he cleared aside the chair and table, and took a brown

soldier's blanket from the tool chest, spreading it slowly. She glanced at his face, as she stood motionless.

His face was pale and without expression, like that of a man submitting to fate.

"You lie there," he said softly, and he shut the door so that it was dark, quite dark.

With a queer obedience, she lay down on the blanket. Then she felt the soft, groping, helplessly desirous hand touching her body, feeling for her face. The hand stroked her face softly, softly, with infinite soothing and assurance, and at last there was the soft touch of a kiss on her cheek.

She lay quite still, in a sort of sleep, in a sort of dream. Then she quivered as she felt his hand groping softly, yet with queer thwarted clumsiness among her clothing. Yet the hand knew, too, how to unclothe her where it wanted. He drew down the thin silk sheath, slowly, carefully, right down and over her feet. Then with a quiver of exquisite pleasure he touched the warm soft body, and touched her navel for a moment in a kiss. And he had to come in to her at once, to enter the peace on earth of her soft, quiescent body. It was the moment of pure peace for him, the entry into the body of the woman.

She lay still, in a kind of sleep, always in a kind of sleep. The activity, the orgasm was his, all his; she could strive for herself no more. Even the tightness of his arms round her, even the intense movement of his body, and the springing of his seed in her, was a kind of sleep, from which she did not begin to rouse till he had finished and lay softly panting against her breast.

Then she wondered, just dimly wondered, why? Why was this necessary? Why had it lifted a great cloud from her and given her peace? Was it real? Was it real?

Her tormented modern-woman's brain still had no rest. Was it real? And she knew, if she gave herself to the man, it was real. But if she kept herself for herself, it was nothing. She was old; millions of years old, she felt. And at last, she could bear the burden of herself no more. She was to be had for the taking. To be had for the taking.

The man lay in a mysterious stillness. What was he feeling? What was he thinking? She did not know. He was a strange man to her; she did not know him. She must only wait, for she did not dare to break his mysterious stillness. He lay there with his arms round her, his body on hers, his wet body touching hers, so close. And completely unknown. Yet not unpeaceful. His very stillness was peaceful.

She knew that, when at last he roused and drew away from her. It was like an abandonment. He drew her dress in the darkness down over her knees and stood a few moments, apparently adjusting his own clothing. Then he quietly opened the door and went out.

She saw a very brilliant little moon shining above the afterglow over the oaks. Quickly she got up and arranged herself; she was tidy. Then she went to the door of the hut.

All the lower wood was in shadow, almost darkness. Yet the sky overhead was crystal. But it shed hardly any light. He came through the lower shadow towards her, his face lifted like a pale blotch.

"Shall we go, then?" he said.

"Where?"

"I'll go with you to the gate."

He arranged things his own way. He locked the door of the hut and came after her.

"You aren't sorry, are you?" he asked, as he went at her side.

"No! No! Are you?" she said.

"For that! No!" he said. Then after a while he added: "But there's the rest of things."

"What rest of things?" she said.

"Sir Clifford. Other folks. All the complications."

"Why complications?" she said, disappointed.

"It's always so. For you as well as for me. There's always complications." He walked on steadily in the dark.

"And are you sorry?" she said.

"In a way!" he replied, looking up at the sky. "I thought I'd done with it all. Now I've begun again."

"Begun what?"

"Life."

"Life!" she re-echoed, with a queer thrill.

"It's life," he said. "There's no keeping clear. And if you do keep clear you might almost as well die. So if I've got to be broken open again, I have."

She did not quite see it that way, but still...

"It's just love," she said cheerfully.

"Whatever that may be," he replied.

They went on through the darkening wood in silence, till they were almost at the gate.

"But you don't hate me, do you?" she said wistfully.

"Nay, nay," he replied. And suddenly he held her fast against his breast again, with the old connecting passion. "Nay, for me it was good, it was good. Was it for you?"

"Yes, for me too," she answered, a little untruthfully, for she had not been conscious of much.

He kissed her softly, softly, with the kisses of warmth.

"If only there weren't so many other people in the world," he said lugubriously.

She laughed. They were at the gate to the park. He opened it for her.

"I won't come any further," he said.

"No!" And she held out her hand, as if to shake hands. But he took it in both his.

"Shall I come again?" she asked wistfully.

"Yes! Yes!"

She left him and went across the park.

This was no casual coupling for Mellors; he is a sensitive thinking man who has had his share of troubles. After saying goodnight to Lady Chatterly, he muses on the way back to his cottage:

He thought with infinite tenderness of the woman. Poor forlorn thing, she was nicer than she knew, and oh! so much too nice for the tough lot she was in contact with. Poor thing, she too had some of the vulnerability of the wild hyacinths, she wasn't all tough rubber-goods and platinum, like the modern girl. And they would do her in! As sure as life, they would do her in, as they do in all naturally tender life. Tender! Somewhere she was tender, tender with a tenderness of the growing hyacinths, something that has

gone out of the celluloid women of today. But he would protect
her with his heart for a little while. For a little while, before the
insentient iron world and the Mammon of mechanized greed did
them both in, her as well as him.

He went home with his gun and his dog, to the dark cottage,
lit the lamp, started the fire, and ate his supper of bread and cheese,
young onions and beer. He was alone, in a silence he loved.

Their next encounter is better for Connie, but still not perfect.

"Let me come in then," he said softly. "An' take off your
mackintosh."

He hung up his gun, slipped out of his wet leather jacket,
and reached for the blankets.

"I brought another blanket," he said, "so we can put one over
us if we like."

"I can't stay long," she said. "Dinner is half-past seven."

He looked at her swiftly, then at his watch.

"All right," he said.

He shut the door, and lit a tiny light in the hanging hurricane lamp.

"One time we'll have a long time," he said.

He put the blankets down carefully, one folded for her head.
Then he sat down a moment on the stool, and drew her to him,
holding her close with one arm, feeling for her body with his free
hand. She heard the catch of his in-taken breath as he found her.
Under her frail petticoat she was naked.

"Eh! what it is to touch thee!" he said, as his finger caressed
the delicate, warm, secret skin of her waist and hips. He put his
face down and rubbed his cheek against her belly and against her
thighs again and again. And again she wondered a little over the
sort of rapture it was to him. She did not understand the beauty
he found in her, through touch upon her living secret body, almost
the ecstasy of beauty. For passion alone is awake to it. And when
passion is dead, or absent, then the magnificent throb of beauty is
incomprehensible and even a little despicable; warm, live beauty
of contact, so much deeper than the beauty of wisdom. She felt
the glide of his cheek on her thighs and belly and buttocks, and

the close brushing of his moustache and his soft thick hair, and her knees began to quiver. Far down in her she felt a new stirring, a new nakedness emerging. And she was half afraid. Half she wished he would not caress her so. He was encompassing her somehow. Yet she was waiting, waiting.

And when he came into her, with an intensification of relief and consummation, that was pure peace to him, still she was waiting. She felt herself a little left out. And she knew, partly it was her own fault. She willed herself into this separateness. Now perhaps she was condemned to it. She lay still, feeling his motion within her, his deep-sunk intentness, the sudden quiver of him at the springing of his seed, then the slow-subsiding thrust. That thrust of the buttocks, surely it was a little ridiculous. If you were a woman, and apart in all the business, surely that thrusting of the man's buttocks was supremely ridiculous. Surely the man was intensely ridiculous in this posture and this act!

But she lay still, without recoil. Even, when he had finished, she did not rouse herself to get a grip on her own satisfaction, as she had done with Michaelis; she lay still, and the tears slowly filled and ran from her eyes.

He lay still, too. But he held her close and tried to cover her poor naked legs with his legs, to keep them warm. He lay on her with a close, undoubting warmth.

"Are you cold?" he asked, in a soft, small voice, as if she were close, so close. Whereas she was left out, distant.

"No! But I must go," she said gently.

He sighed, held her closer, then relaxed to rest again.

He had not guessed her tears. He thought she was there with him.

"I must go," she repeated.

He lifted himself, kneeled beside her a moment, kissed the inner side of her thighs, then drew down her skirts, buttoning his own clothes unthinking, not even turning aside, in the faint, faint light from the lantern.

"Tha mun come ter th' cottage one time," he said, looking down at her with a warm, sure, easy face.

But she lay there inert, and was gazing up at him thinking. Stranger! Stranger! She even resented him a little.

He put on his coat and looked for his hat, which had fallen, then he slung on his gun.

"Come then!" he said, looking down at her with those warm, peaceful sort of eyes.

She rose slowly. She didn't want to go. She also rather resented staying. He helped her with her thin waterproof, and saw she was tidy.

Then he opened the door. The outside was quite dark. The faithful dog under the porch stood up with pleasure seeing him. The drizzle of rain drifted greyly past under the darkness. It was quite dark.

"Ah mua ta'e th' lantern," he said. "The'll be nob'dy."

He walked just before her in the narrow path, swinging the hurricane lamp low, revealing the wet grass, the black shiny tree roots like snakes, wan flowers. For the rest, all was grey rain-mist and complete darkness.

"Tha mun come to the cottage one time," he said, "shall ta? We might as well be hung for a sheep as for a lamb."

It puzzled her, his queer, persistent wanting her, when there was nothing between them, when he never really spoke to her, and in spite of herself she resented the dialect. His "tha mun come" seemed not addressed to her, but some common woman.

Because of the watershed importance of Lawrence's novel, it deserves this maze of space herein.

This is the account of their third copulation, and Connie finally achieves nirvana:

She started out of her muse, and gave a little cry of fear. A man was there.

It was the keeper, he stood in the path like Balaam's ass, barring her way.

"How's this?" he said in surprise.

"How did you come?" she panted.

"How did you? Have you been to the hut?"

"No! No! I went to Marehay."

He looked at her curiously, searchingly, and she hung her head a little guiltily.

"And were you going to the hut now?" he asked rather sternly.

"No! I mustn't, I stayed at Marehay. No one knows where I am. I'm late. I've got to run."

"Giving me the slip, like?" he said, with a faint ironic smile.

"No! No. Not that. Only—"

"Why, what else?" he said. And he stepped up to her, and put his arm around her. She felt the front of his body terribly near to her, and alive.

"Oh, not now, not now," she cried, trying to push him away.

"Why not? It's only six o'clock. You've got half an hour. Nay! Nay! I want you."

He held her fast and she felt his urgency. Her old instinct was to fight for her freedom. But something else in her was strange and inert and heavy. His body was urgent against her, and she hadn't the heart any more to fight.

He looked round.

"Come—come here! Through here," he said, looking penetratingly into the dense fir trees, that were young and not more than half-grown.

He looked back at her. She saw his eyes, tense and brilliant, fierce, not loving. But her will had left her. A strange weight was on her limbs. She was giving way. She was giving up.

He led her through the wall of prickly trees, that were difficult to come through, to a place where there was a little space and a pile of dead boughs. He threw one or two dry ones down, put his coat and waistcoat over them, and she had to lie down there under the boughs of the tree, like an animal, while he waited, standing there in his shirt and breeches, watching her with haunted eyes. But still he was provident—he made her lie properly, properly. Yet he broke the band of her underclothes, for she did not help him, only lay inert.

He too had bared the front part of his body and she felt his naked flesh against her as he came in to her. For a moment he was still inside her, turgid there and quivering. Then as he began to move, in the sudden helpless orgasm, there awoke in her new strange thrills rippling inside her. Rippling, rippling, rippling, like a flapping overlapping of soft flames, soft as feathers, running to points of brilliance, exquisite, exquisite and melting her all molten inside. It was like bells rippling up and up to a culmination. She lay unconscious of the wild little cries she uttered at the last. But it was over too soon, too soon, and she could no longer force her own conclusion with her own activity. This was different, different. She could do nothing. She could no longer harden and grip for her own satisfaction upon him. She could only wait, wait and moan in spirit as she felt him withdrawing, withdrawing and contracting, coming to the terrible moment when he would slip out of her and be gone. Whilst all her womb was open and soft, and softly clamouring, like a sea-anemone under the tide, clamouring for him to come in again and make a fulfillment for her. She clung to him unconscious in passion, and he never quite slipped from her, and she felt the soft bud of him within her stirring, and strange rhythms flushing up into her with a strange rhythmic growing motion, swelling and swelling till it filled her all cleaving consciousness, and then began again the unspeakable motion that was not really motion, but pure deepening whirlpools of sensation swirling deeper and deeper through all her tissue and consciousness, till she was one perfect concentric fluid of feeling, and she lay there crying in unconscious inarticulate cries. The voice out of the uttermost night, the life! The man heard it beneath him with a kind of awe, as his life sprang out into her. And as it subsided, he subsided too and lay utterly still, unknowing, while her grip on him slowly relaxed, and she lay inert. And they lay and knew nothing, not even of each other, both lost. Till at last he began to rouse and become aware of his defenseless nakedness, and she was aware that his body was loosening its clasp on her. He was coming apart; but in her breast she felt she could not bear him to leave her uncovered. He must cover her now for ever.

The novel is about two lonely and spiritually dead people who are brought back to life by the love which is found through sex.

I don't think it will spoil the story for anyone who has not read the novel to learn that things work out well for the lovers. Mellors drops the accent and the peasant pose, Connie gets pregnant by him, and they plan to get married as soon as possible. The famous final page of the novel is a letter from Mellors to Connie which ends:

"Now I can't even leave off writing to you.

"But a great deal of us is together, and we can but abide by it, and steer our courses to meet soon. John Thomas says good night to Lady Jane, a little droopingly, but with a hopeful heart."

(Lady Jane and John Thomas are the couples' nicknames for their private parts.)

One of the most talked about scenes of the book was this bucolic episode:

> He fetched columbines and campions and new-mown hay and oak tufts and honeysuckle in small bud. He fastened fluffy young oak sprigs round her breasts and in her navel he poised a pink campion flower and in her maiden-hair were forget-me-nots and wood ruff. And he stuck flowers in the hair of his own body and wound a bit of creeping jenny round his penis and stuck a single bell of hyacinth in his navel. 'This is John Thomas marrying Lady Jane', he said.

The book was praised and derided and parodied ("Lady Loverly's Chatter," etc.) A parody published in the *New Yorker* magazine in 1932 begins as follows:

> Lady Constance Chatterly had got her divorce from Sir Clifford Chatterly. She and Mellors, the gamekeeper, had married, had come out to America, and were living in sin just outside Philadelphia. It was six o'clock of a chilly autumn morning.
>
> "Are ye awake, lass?" murmured Mellors. He still had his Yorkshire burr.
>
> "No," said Connie.
>
> She knew what he wanted. He wanted her to get up and close the window. Sure enough:
>
> "Wi' ye git up and close the winna, mayhap?" he suggested.

And so the parody goes forth. And then:

> The morning light caught Mellors' flank and it gleamed. Connie gazed at it. She sighed.

She remembered the morning following that first night she had spent at Mellors' cottage up by the fen, just across the lea, and down by the downs. She minded how she had lain abed and watched his glistening flank as he strode across the room to close the window. The old Mellors flank had changed a lot in the year. Or had she changed? Why was his flank always glistening, anyhow? It's all right, thought Connie, for a flank to glisten once in a while. I'm broad-minded, she told herself, I'd be the last girl in the world to condemn flank-glistening, but...Oh Lord, flanks ain't no treat to me, thought Connie. Not any more.

Yes, it was easy to make nervous sport of Lawrence's style, but the novel was, and is, a milestone for freedom of expression of any sort for the writer.

If you don't want to read a "dirty book"—just don't.

6

Lolita

"I don't wish to touch hearts, I don't even want to
affect minds very much. What I really want to produce
is that little sob in the spine of the artist-reader."
Vladimir Nabokov

ANOTHER GREAT LANDMARK IN THE REALM OF SEXUAL LITERATURE
appeared on the scene some twenty-seven years after *Lady Chatterly's
Lover*. *Lolita* was written in 1953 in English—superb, dazzling English—
by the Russian novelist, Vladimir Nabokov. It is the strange, comic-tragic
tale told by a middle-aged, sophisticated Humbert Humbert about his
blind, obsessive love for Dolores Haze, a twelve-year-old American
"nymphet," a rather nasty, self-centered girl. Humbert marries her mother
to get closer to the girl, and when the mother is killed in a car accident, he
takes his Lolita on an aimless hegira around America. There is mayhem
and murder but all related with a comic and ironic feel to the writing.

In spite of its brilliance, several publishers turned the book down, and
it wasn't until 1955 that 5,000 copies were published in Paris. They were
gobbled up. It was immediately condemned in England—("the filthiest
book ever written")—but was finally published in 1958 in America. It
became the first novel since *Gone With the Wind* to sell 100,000 copies in
the first three weeks of publication. In 1998, the Modern Library named
it "the fourth greatest English language novel of the twentieth century."

Though Humbert's perverted lust permeates the novel, there are
few explicit sex scenes. One does occur when Humbert thinks back to

the first love of his youth, another nymphet, named Annabel, who was
to die young:

> She trembled and twitched as I kissed the corner of her parted
> lips and the hot lobe of her ear. A cluster of stars palely glowed
> above us, between the silhouettes of long thin leaves; that vibrant
> sky seemed as naked as she was under her light frock. I saw her face
> in the sky, strangely distinct, as if it emitted a faint radiance of its
> own. Her legs, her lovely live legs, were not too close together, and
> when my hand located what it sought, a dreamy and eerie expres-
> sion, half-pleasure, half-pain, came over those childish features. She
> sat a little higher than I, and whenever in her solitary ecstasy she
> was led to kiss me, her head would bend with a sleepy, soft, droop-
> ing movement that was almost woeful, and her bare knees caught
> and compressed my wrist, and slackened again; and her quivering
> mouth, distorted by the acridity of some mysterious potion, with
> a sibilant intake of breath came near to my face. She would try to
> relieve the pain of love by first roughly rubbing her dry lips against
> mine; then my darling would draw away with a nervous toss of
> her hair, and then again come darkly near and let me feed on her
> open mouth, while with a generosity that was ready to offer her
> everything, my heart, my throat, my entrails, I have her to hold
> in her awkward fist the scepter of my passion.

Not until the middle of the novel is there a sexual encounter between
Humbert and Lolita. They are traveling about America in the guise of
father and step-daughter and are forced to share a bed in a crowded hotel.
He lusts after her during the night but makes no overtures. In the morning
however, the following scene unfolds:

> I had thought that months, perhaps years, would elapse before
> I dared to reveal myself to Dolores Haze; but by six she was wide
> awake, and by six fifteen we were technically lovers. I am going
> to tell you something very strange: it was she who seduced me.
> All at once, with a burst of rough glee (the sign of the
> nymphet!), she put her mouth to my ear—but for quite a while
> my mind could not separate into words the hot thunder of her
> whisper, and she laughed, and brushed the hair off her face, and

tried again, and gradually the odd sense of living in a brand new, mad new dream world, where everything was permissible, came over me as I realized what she was suggesting. I answered I did not know what game she and Charlie had played. "You mean you have never—?"—her features twisted into a stare of disgusted incredulity. "You have never—" she started again. I took time out by nuzzling her a little. "Lay off, will you," she said with a twangy whine, hastily removing her brown shoulder from my lips. (It was very curious the ways she considered—and kept doing so for a long time——all caresses except kisses on the mouth or the stark act of love either "romantic slosh" or "abnormal.")

"You mean," she persisted, now kneeling above me, "you never did it when you were a kid?"

"Never," I answered, quite truthful.

"Okay," said Lolita, "here is where we start."

However, I shall not bore my learned readers with a detailed account of Lolita's presumption. Suffice it to say that not a trace of modesty did I perceive in this beautiful hardly formed young girl whom modern co-education, juvenile mores, the campfire racket and so forth had utterly and hopelessly depraved. She saw the stark act merely as part of a youngster's furtive world, unknown to adults. What adults did for purposes of procreation was no business of hers.

Humbert, a master of self deception, states:

> If I dwell at some length on the tremors and gropings of that distant night, it is because I insist upon proving that I am not, and never was, and never could have been, a brutal scoundrel. The gentle and dreamy regions through which I crept were the patrimonies of poets—*not* crime's prowling ground.

Much has been written about *Lolita*. One interesting analysis by the late Canadian novelist, Robertson Davies, claims that the theme of *Lolita* is "not the corruption of an innocent child by a cunning adult, but the exploitation of a weak adult by a corrupt child."

In 1958, Lionel Trilling warned of the moral difficulty in interpreting a book with so eloquent and so self-deceived a narrator, Humbert himself. Trilling commented: "We find ourselves the more shocked when we realize that in the course of reading the novel, we have come virtually to condone the violation it presents—we have been seduced into conniving in the violation because we have permitted our fantasies to accept what we know to be revolting."

Martin Amis has written of the novel:

> Human beings laugh, if you notice, to express relief, exaspera-
> tion, stoicism, hysteria, embarrassment, disgust and cruelty. *Lolita*
> is perhaps the funniest novel in the language because it allows
> laughter its full complexity and range.

Such is the power of Nabokov's writing. Excerpts from the work cannot do this masterpiece justice, and certainly the two films made from it didn't come close. But, by reading *Lolita*, a would-be writer can learn how to write a beautiful, sex-driven novel with no gross language or uncomfortable images.

7

"Hah-Hah,
Was It Funny for You, Too?"

The pleasure is momentary, the position ridiculous,
and the expense damnable.
Lord Chesterfield

THERE IS SO MUCH WRITING ABOUT SEX THAT OF COURSE IT HAS
been the source of a lot of comedy, low and high and in-between.

Peter Mathiessen's wonderful 1965 novel, *At Play in the Fields of
the Lord*, is serious and suspenseful, but it has its comic moments. For
example, Moon and Wolfie, as soldiers of fortune, are flying low over a
Brazilian Amazon Indian village; Moon is the pilot. A native shoots an
arrow at the plane, but Wolfie is determined to finish his story of how he
first got together with Azusa, his wife back in New York. Moon is busy
flying the plane.

> He circled closer, banking low; he could scarcely hope to
> glimpse the Niaruna, and he was about to climb again when he
> saw what he had come down to this continent to see. A naked man
> appeared at the edge of the clearing, and stamping violently on
> the ground, raised a black bow. Moon did not see the arrow until
> it hung suspended for an instant at the top of its arc: a gleam of
> blue-and-yellow feathering, like a small bird, a turn of dull light
> on the cane shift...

"...like, one problem," Wolfie was saying, "was getting her to be, you know, like *in*timate. Man, I tried everythin, even daisies. Finely I grabbed her hand and *put* it there—it didn't take. It got to be this kind of a joke: her sayin she would never touch me, I was too funky, man, I was not her type, Azusa said. Well, I was kind of, you know, like intrigued. So I got her to promise just one little thing: If you ever touch it, Zoose, I says, just even once, then we go all the way—right, baby?"

And then:

The bright shimmer of the arrow, the lone naked figure howling at the sky—it had been years since he had grinned like that, with all his lungs and heart; he actually yipped in sheer delight. Now he had sensed something unnamable and always known, something glimpsed, hinted at, withheld by sun and wind, by the enormous sky...

"What are you, airsick? You got this awful look on your face, you're makin noises!" Wolfie shrugged, and clasped his hands behind his head. "Anyway, Old Azusa knew that I meant business, see, like she grown wary. And I was gonna give up hope on her, and was kickin myself for getting hung up on a chick that was sexually disturbed, when one night we was sittin in this art film, eatin popcorn outta the same box, and she says, 'Did you find the prize yet? This popcorn got these little prizes, see.' Well, like instantly I get this beautiful idea from this joke that I heard it once, but beautiful, the answer to a maiden's prayer. As usual I had, you know, this erection, so quick as a mink I work a hole through the bottom of the box, with my fingers, I mean, and insert it, you know, all sweet and innocent, nestling right up amongst these popcorns, dig? Then I whispers, 'No, Zoose, dear, I didn't find it yet, I'll race you.' Well, Old Azusa digs right in Old Azusa knew that I meant business she's still watchin this art film, see Old Azusa knew that I meant business and whammo! 'What the hell kind of corn d'you call this?' She yells. 'It's livin! That's the prize,' I says to her, 'that them popcorn people laid on you, like maybe it's some nutty kind of a pet.' Well, you know, man, that crazy chick Old Azusa knew that I meant business—once she got hold of it she never let go for a week, and it was exactly nine months after this art film that we gave birth to this infint which we named it Dick..."

Many, many pages and adventures later, Wolfie is still in the jungle. He writes a clumsy but touching letter to Azusa.

Moon wasn't coming back, and that was that. The diamonds would take him home. But first maybe he would write Azusa and find out where home was these days. Right now, Wolfie said fiercely, and he sprang up and ran out to find paper, feeling decisive for the first time in months.

Dear Azusa –
This is me. Did you think I was dead? Ha, ha. Where are you living at. I am writing care of your mother, tell the old fart Hello (like hell). Zoose, I miss you and Dick, I am awful lonely, and if you will just let me know where are you living at I will come on home and settle down a while, all right? Don't be sore at me, by-gones are bygones, baby, right? I am kind of tired and lonely, like I said. Remember that time in the art movie I fooled you with that popcorn? Ha, ha. Well, baby, keep it hot for me, you always were a swinger, Zoose. Like maybe you been doing a few tricks on the side since I was gone—well, that's okay, I mean, who hasn't, right? Forgive and forget, okay, Zoose?
So how is Dick? He ain't no infint anymore, I bet. Since I last seen him, I been shot at in the Congo, Cuba—all over—and I'm just as broke and stupid as I ever was! Well we had some laughs, though, wait til I get home and tell you, you will break up. Only now my partner got hung up on some local kind of junk and went and got killed on me and crashed our aircraft along with it, and without him it ain't a funny scene no more. Because before this happened, him and me made a lot of very comical scenes which I will save them to tell you when I get home. Write quick to the address below and let me know where are you at.
Your wandering Jewish boy and common-law husband,
Wolfie

If you saw the film, or *especially* if you saw the disappointing film, you would enjoy this exciting and rich novel.

Charles Johnson's *Middle Passage* won the 1990 National Book Award. The following gentle, awkward, and droll encounter is from that novel.

Isadora speaks:

"Are those flowers for me?" she asked. Again, she flashed that foolish, fetching, teasingly erotic smile. "Bring them here."

I sat down beside her, kissed the cheek she turned up toward me, than sat twiddling my thumbs. Meanwhile, Isadora took a whiff of the flowers strong enough to suck a few petals into her nose. She let the bouquet fall to the floor and turned to me after moistening her lips with the tip of her tongue. Placing her left hand on my shoulder to hold me still, she used her right to grip the top of my slops, and pulled. Buttons popped off my breeches like buckshot, pinging against the bulkhead.

"Isadora," I asked in a pinched voice, "are you sure you want to do this? We can sit and read Scripture or poetry together, if you wish."

She made answer by rising to her bare feet, shoving me back onto the bed, and tugging off my boots and breeches. By heaven, I thought, still water runs deep. Who'd have dreamed these depths of passion were in a prim Boston schoolteacher? She was so sexually bold I began to squirm. I mean, I was the sailor, wasn't I? Abruptly, my own ache for detumescence, for a little Late Night All Right, took hold of me, beginning at about my fourth rib and flying downward. Soon we both had our hands inside each other's clothes. How long it had been since someone held me, touched me with something other than a boot heel or the back of their hand! And she, so much slimmer—pulling the gown over her head—was to me a figure of such faint inducing grace any Odysseus would have swallowed the ocean whole, if need be, to swim to her side. I kissed the swale by her collarbone and trailed my lips along her neck. Then, afraid of what I might do next, I slid my fingers under my thighs and sat on my hands.

Isadora twirled slowly on her toes, letting me see all of her. Now that she had my undivided attention, she asked, "Well, what do you think?"

"I'm not thinking."

"Good."

"But the animals. Can't you send them outside?"

"Rutherford!"

"At least cover up the birdcage."

"Don't worry, he's blind." Her voice was husky. "Just lie still."

Knowing nothing else to do, I obeyed. Isadora climbed over my outstretched legs, lowered herself to my waist, and began pushing her hips back and forth, whispering. "No, don't move." I wondered: Where did she learn this? Against her wishes, I did move, easing her onto her side, then placed my hand where it wanted to go. We groped awkwardly for a while, but something was wrong. Things were not progressing as smoothly as they were supposed to. ("Your elbow's in my eyeball," said I; "Sorry," said she; "Hold on, I think I've got a charley horse.") I was out of practice. Rusty. My body's range of motion was restricted by the bruises I had taken at sea, yet my will refused to let go. I peeled off my blouse, determined to lay the ax to the root like a workman spitting on his palms before settling down to the business at hand; but, hang it, my memories of the Middle Passage kept coming back, reducing the velocity of my desire, its violence, and in place of my longing for feverish love-making left only a vast stillness that felt remarkably full, a feeling that, just now, I wanted our futures blended, not our limbs, our histories perfectly twined for all time, not our flesh.

From the genteel to the totally ridiculous, consider Wilt, the protagonist of the novel of the same name. Never has a reader been asked to accept a fictional premise and situation of such an unbelievable scene, and yet we are being seduced by a good writer, and we do accept and believe that stuffy, proper Wilt somehow got into the sort of sexual, well, impossible *unpleasantness* that befalls him.

In this 1976 novel, *Wilt,* by the English author Tom Sharpe, the eponymous mousy professor is at a cocktail party given by Gaskell, a colleague. Sally, the host's sexy wife, is flirting with Wilt while his own wife, Eva, is in the kitchen with the other guests.

They went upstairs and down a passage to a small bedroom filled with toys. There was a model train set on the floor, a punch bag, an enormous Teddy Bear, a rocking horse, a fireman's helmet and a life-size inflated doll that looked like a real woman.

"That's Judy," said Sally, "she's got a real cunt. Gaskell is a plastic freak." Wilt winced. "And here are Gaskell's toys. Puberty baby."

Wilt looked round the room at the mess and shook his head. "Looks as though he's making up for a lost childhood," he said.

"Oh, Henry, you're so perceptive," said Sally, and unscrewed the top of the Vodka bottle.

"I'm not. It's just bloody obvious."

"Oh you are. You're just terribly modest, is all. Modest and shy and manly." She swigged from the bottle and gave it to Wilt. He took a mouthful inadvisedly and had trouble swallowing it. Sally locked the door and sat down on the bed. She reached up a hand and pulled Wilt towards her.

"Screw me, Henry baby," she said and lifted her skirt, "fuck me, honey. Screw the pants off me."

"That," said Wilt, "would be a bit difficult."

"Oh. Why?"

"Well for one thing you don't appear to be wearing any and anyway why should I?"

"You want a reason? A reason for screwing?"

"Yes," said Wilt. "Yes I do."

Sally pulled down her skirt and sat up.

"You won't?"

"No," said Wilt.

"Are you a bondage baby? You can tell me. I'm used to bondage babies. Gaskell is real..."

"Certainly not," said Wilt. "I don't care what Gaskell is."

"You want a blow job, is that it? You want for me to give you a blow job?" She got off the bed and came towards him. Wilt looked at her wildly.

"Don't you touch me," he shouted, his mind alive with images of burning paint. "I don't want anything from you."

Sally stopped and stared at him. She wasn't smiling any more.

"Why not? Because you're small? Is that why?"

Wilt backed against the door.

"No, it isn't."

"Because you haven't the courage of your instincts? Because you're a psychic virgin? Because you're not a man? Because you can't take a woman who thinks?"

"Thinks?" yelled Wilt, stung into action by the accusation that he wasn't a man. "Thinks? You think? You know something? I'd rather have it off with that plastic mechanical doll than you. It's got more sex appeal in its little finger than you have in your whole rotten body. When I want a whore I'll buy one."

"Why you little shit," said Sally, and lunged at him. Wilt scuttled sideways and collided with the punch bag. The next moment he had stepped on a model engine and was hurtling across the room. As he slumped down the wall on to the floor, Sally picked up the doll and leaned over him.

When Wilt comes to, he finds himself in the bizarre plight his vengeful hostess has put him into:

Upstairs in the toy room, Wilt, recovering slowly from the combined assaults on his system of Pringsheim Punch, vodka, his nymphomaniac hostess, and the corner of the cupboard against which he had fallen, had the feeling that something was terribly wrong. It wasn't simply that the room was oscillating, that he had a lump on the back of his head, or that he was naked. It was rather the sensation that something with all the less attractive qualities of a mousetrap, or a vice, or a starving clam, had attached itself implacably to what he had up till now always considered to be the most private of his parts. Wilt opened his eyes and found himself staring into a smiling if slightly swollen face. He shut his eyes again, hoped against hope, opened them again, found the face still there and made an effort to sit up.

It was an unwise move. Judy, the plastic doll, inflated beyond her normal pressure, resisted. With a squawk, Wilt fell back on to the floor. Judy followed. Her nose bounced on his face and her breasts on his chest. With a curse, Wilt rolled on to his side and considered the problem. Sitting up was out of the question. That way led to castration. He would have to try something else. He rolled the doll over further and climbed on top only to decide that his weight on it was increasing the pressure on what remained of his penis and that if he wanted to get gangrene that was the way to go about getting it. Wilt rolled off precipitately and groped for a valve. There must be one somewhere, if he could only find it. But if there was a valve it was well hidden and by the feel of things he hadn't got time to waste finding it. He felt round on the floor for something to use as a dagger, something sharp, and finally broke off a piece of railway track and plunged it into his assailant's back. There was a squeak of plastic but Judy's swollen smile remained unchanged and her unwanted attentions as implacable as ever. Again and again, he stabbed her but to no avail. Wilt dropped his makeshift dagger and considered other means. He was getting frantic, conscious of a new threat. It was no longer that he was the subject of her high air pressure. His own internal pressures were mounting. The Pringsheim Punch and the vodka were making their presence felt. With a desperate thought that if he didn't get out of here soon he would burst, Wilt seized Judy's head, bent it sideways and sank his teeth into her neck. Or [he] would have had her pounds per square inch permitted. Instead he bounced off and spent the next two minutes trying to find his false tooth which had been dislodged in the exchange.

By the time he had got it back in place, panic had set in. He had to get out of the doll. He just had to.

Poor Wilt doesn't know it, but his troubles have just begun.

Nelson deMille, author of dozens of super suspense thrillers like *The Charm School*, also likes to inject some sex and games into his novels, like this very unusual sex scene in his 1990 best seller, *The Gold Coast*:

I saw now a white horse nibbling on new spring grass between two toppled columns. Astride the horse was the familiar figure of a woman dressed in tight jeans and a black turtleneck sweater. She turned to me as I approached, then faced away. It was my wife, Susan, but I could tell from her look that she was not herself. What I mean is, she likes to playact. So, to be cooperative, I called out, "Who are you?"

She turned back to me and responded in an icy voice, "Who are you?"

Actually, I wasn't sure yet, but I improvised. "I own this land," I said. "Are you lost or trespassing?"

"Neither. And I doubt anyone dressed as you are, with so wretched a horse, could own this land."

"Don't be insolent. Are you alone?"

"I was until you came by," she retorted.

I pulled in Yankee side by side with the white Arabian. "What is *your* name?"

"Daphne. What is *your* name?"

I still couldn't think of a name for me, so I said, "You should know whose land you are on. Get down from your horse."

"Why should I?"

"Because I said so. And if you don't, I'll pull you down and take my switch to you. Dismount!"

She hesitated, then dismounted.

"Tether him."

She tethered her horse to a cherry limb and stood facing me.

"Take off your clothes."

She shook her head. "I won't."

"You will," I snapped. "Quickly."

She stood motionless a moment, then pulled off her turtleneck, exposing two firm breasts. She stood with the sweater in her hand and looked up at me. "Do I have to do this?"

"Yes."

She dropped the sweater, then pulled off her boots and socks. Finally she slid her jeans and panties off and threw them in the grass.

I sidled my horse closer and looked down at her standing naked in the fading sunlight. "Not so arrogant now, are you, Daphne?"

"No, sir."

This is Susan's idea of keeping marital sex interesting, though to be honest, I'm not complaining about acting out Susan's sexual fantasies. Sometimes these dramas are scripted and directed (by Susan); sometimes as with this encounter, they are improv. The locales change with the seasons; in the winter we do it in the stable or, to relive our youth, in front of a fireplace in a deserted mansion.

This was our first alfresco encounter of the new spring season, and there is something about a woman standing naked in a field or forest that appeals to the most primal instincts of both sexes, while at the same time flouting modern conventions regarding where love should be made. Trust me on this; you get used to the occasional ant or bumblebee.

Susan asked, "What are you going to do to me?"

"Whatever I wish." I looked at Susan standing motionless, her long red hair blowing in strands across her face, waiting patiently for a command. She has no acting background, but if she had, she would be a method actress; there was not a hint in her face or bearing that she was my wife and that this was a game. For all purposes, she was a naked, defenseless woman who was about to be raped by a strange man on horseback. In fact, her knees were shaking, and she seemed honestly frightened.

"Please, sir, do what you will with me, but do it quickly."

I'm not good at the impromptu games, and I'd rather she scripted it so I know who I'm supposed to be or at least what historical epoch we're in. Sometimes I'm a Roman or a barbarian, a knight or an aristocrat, and she's a slave, a peasant, or a haughty noblewoman who gets her comeuppance.

I brought Yankee right up to Susan and reached out and held her upraised chin in my hand. "Are you embarrassed?"

"Yes, sir."

I should mention that Susan often takes the dominant role, and I'm the one who plays the part of a naked slave at auction or a prisoner who is stripped and given a few lashes, or whatever. Lest you think we are utterly depraved, I want you to know we are both registered Republicans and members of the Episcopal Church, and attend regularly except during the boating season.

Anyway, on this occasion, I had the feeling we were in the seventeenth century or thereabouts, thus the "Don't be insolent" line and all the rest of the silly dialogue. I tried to think of another great line and finally said, "Are you Daphne, wife of the traitor Sir John Worthington?"

"I am, sir. And if you are indeed Lord Hardwick, I've come to ask you to intercede on my husband's behalf with his Majesty, the King."

I was indeed hardwick at that moment and wished I'd worn looser trousers. "I am every inch Hardwick," I replied, and saw a real smile flit across her face.

Susan dropped to her knees and wrapped her arms around my boot. "Oh, please, my lord, you must present my petition to King Charles."

History is not my strong point, but I can usually wing it. History wasn't the point anyway. I said, "And what favor will you do me in return if I do this for you?"

"I will do *anything* you wish."

That was the point. And in truth, the playacting usually got me jump-started before Susan, and I wanted to get on with the last scene. "Stand," I commanded.

She stood and I grabbed her wrist as I took my foot from the stirrup. "Put your right foot in the stirrup."

She put her bare foot in the stirrup, and I pulled her up facing me, both of us tight in the English saddle, with her arms around me and her bare breasts tight against my chest. I gave Yankee a tap, and he began to walk. I said, "Take it out."

She unzipped my fly and took it out, holding it in her warm hands. I said, "Put it in."

She sobbed and said, "I do this only to save my husband's life. He is the only man I have ever known."

A few clever replies ran through my mind, but the hormones were in complete control of my intellect now, and I snapped, "Put it in!"

She rose up and came down on it, letting out an exclamation of surprise.

"Hold on." I kicked Yankee, and he began to trot. Susan held me tighter and locked her strong legs over mine. She buried her face in my neck, and as the horse bounced along, she moaned. This was not acting.

I was not completely caught up in the heat of the moment. I'm only a fair horseman, and what little skill I have was not equal to this. Yankee trotted at a nice pace through the cherry grove, then out into the pasture. The air was heavy with the smell of horse, the trodden earth, our bodies, and Susan's musky odor rising between us.

God, what a ride, Susan breathing hard on my neck, crying out, me panting, and the wetness oozing between us.

Susan climaxed first and cried out so loudly she flushed a pheasant from a bush. I climaxed a second later and involuntarily jerked on the reins, causing Yankee to nearly tumble.

The horse settled down and began to graze, as if nothing had happened. Susan and I clung to each other, trying to catch our breath. I finally managed to say, "Whew...what a ride..."

Susan smiled. "I'm sorry I trespassed on your land, sir."

"I lied. It's not my land."

"That's all right. I don't have a husband in trouble with the King, either."

We both laughed.

I don't believe we have ever read a sex scene quite like that one, quite an acknowledgment in itself.

A warning is hereby issued: Reading the following may spoil your enjoyment of any *serious* sex scene you may read afterwards. You certainly will never read a description of an orgasm the same way again. You may not even have one the same way again.

This excerpt is from Anthony Burgess's 1965 novel, *Tremor of Intent*, a secret service tale gone mad, a send-up of every James Bond-type book ever written. Burgess (*A Clockwork Orange*, etcetera etcetera) is such a good writer that at first he lulls you into thinking this is a serious approach to the classic international espionage story.

And then along comes this sex scene and you realize you've been had by a master.

An aging British agent based in Yugoslavia, Hillier is sent, with the bribe of a fat retirement bonus, to bring back to England his old school friend Roper, who has become one of the great scientific brains of the USSR. The setting is a cruise ship, moored at a Black Sea port. The ingredients are sex, gluttony, violence, and treachery.

Hillier padded to Cabin No. 58. As he had expected, the door was not locked. He knocked and at once entered. Again as he had expected, Miss Devi said: "You're late."

"Delayed," gulped Hillier, Miss Devi was lying on her bunk, naked except for her silver nose-ring. "Unavoidably." She had loosened her hair and her body was framed in it as far as the knees. Her body was superb, brown as though cooked, with the faintest shimmer of a glaze upon it; the jet-black bush answered the magnificent hair like a cheeky parody; the breasts, though full, did not loll but sat firmly as though moulded out of some celestial rubber; the nipples had already started upright. She reached out her arms, golden swords, towards him. He kicked off his slippers and let his bathrobe fall to the floor. "The light," he gasped, "I must put out the—"

"Leave it on. I want to see."

Hillier engaged. "*Araikkul va,*" she whispered. Tamil? A southern woman then, Dravidian not Aryan. She had been trained out of some manual, but it was not that coarse *Kama Sutra.* Was it the rare book called *Pokam,* whose title Hillier had always re-membered for its facetious English connotation? What now began was agonizingly exquisite, something he had forgotten existed. She gently inflamed him with the *mayil,* or peacock embrace, moved on to the *matakatham,* the *poththi,* the *putani.* Hillier started to pass out of time, nodding to himself as he saw himself begin to take flight. Goodbye, Hillier. A voice beyond, striking like light, humorously catechized him, and he knew all the answers. Holy Cross Day? The festival of the exaltation of the Cross, September 14th. The year of the publication of *Hypatia*? 1853. The Mulready Envelope, The Morall Philosophie of Doni, the Kennington Oval laid out in 1845. The White Doe of Rylstone, Markheim, Thrawn Janet, Wade's magic boat called Wingelock, Pontius Pilate's porter was named Cartaphilus the wandering Jew. When did Queen Elizabeth come to the throne? November, 1558. Something there tried to tug him back, some purpose on earth, connected with now, his job, but he was drawn on and on, beyond, to the very source of the voice. He saw the lips moving, opening as to devour him. The first is the fifth and the fifth is the eighth, he was told by a niggling earth-voice, but he shouted it down. He let himself be lipped in by the chewing mouth, then was masticated strongly till he was resolved into a juice, willing this, wanting it. *Mani, mani* was the word, he remembered. The *mani* was tipped, gallons of it, into a vessel that throbbed as if it were organic and alive, and then the vessel was sealed with hot wax. He received his instructions in the name of man, addressed as Johnrobertjameswilliam (the brothers Maryburgh playing a fife over Pompeii, Spalato, Kenwood, Osterley) Bedebellblair: *Cast forth doughtily!* So to cast forth in that one narrow sweet cave would be to wreck all the ships of the world—*Alabama, Ark, Beagle, Bellerophon, Bounty, Cutty Sark, Dreadnought, Endeavour, Erebus, Fram, Golden Hind, Great Eastern, Great Harry, Marie Celeste, Mayflower, Revenge, Skidbladnir, Victory.* But it was the one way to refertilise all the earth, for the cave opened into myriad channels below ground, mapped before him like the tree of man in an *Anatomy.* The gallons of *mani* had swollen to a scalding ocean on which navies cheered, their masts cracking. The eight-foot tower that crowed from his loins glowed white hot and then disintegrated into a million flying bricks. He pumped the massive burden out. Uriel, Raphael, Raguel, Michael, Sariel, Gabriel and Jerahmeel cried with sevenfold main voice, a common chord that was yet seven distinct and different notes. But, miracle, at once, from unknown reservoirs, the vessel began to fill again.

And on and on it goes, page after page, for those who can take it.

We next move away from all this verbosity and leisurely sexual interludes to the fast and furious—The Quickie.

Brief Encounters

THE SEXUAL QUICKIE SCENE HAS BEEN AROUND IN LITERATURE FOR a long time. I guess my favorite one comes at the ending of a Peter De Vries novel where the hero is dragging the heroine towards the bedroom and she protests:

> "Wait—what about the foreplay?"
> "Later," he pants. "Later!"

THE END

Almost as pithy is the memorable scene in Mario Puzo's 1969 novel, *The Godfather*. But it *is* sexy, and there would appear to be a dearth of foreplay.

There is a huge festive gathering at the Corleone compound for Connie Corleone's wedding. Lucy Mancini is Connie's maid of honor and for some time she has had a yen for Connie's brother, Sonny.

> Lucy Mancini lifted her pink gown off the floor and ran up the steps. Sonny Corleone's heavy Cupid face, redly obscene with winey lust, frightened her, but she had teased him for the past week to just this end. In her two college love affairs she had felt nothing and neither of them lasted more than a week. Quarreling, her second lover had mumbled something about her being "too big down there." Lucy had understood and for the rest of the school term had refused to go out on any dates.

During the summer, preparing for the wedding of her best friend, Connie Corleone, Lucy heard the whispered stories about Sonny. One Sunday afternoon in the Corleone kitchen, Sonny's wife Sandra gossiped freely. Sandra was a coarse, good-natured woman who had been born in Italy but brought to America as a small child. She was strongly built with great breasts and had already borne three children in five years of marriage. Sandra and the other women teased Connie about the terrors of the nuptial bed. "My God," Sandra had giggled, "when I saw that pole of Sonny's for the first time and realized he was going to stick it into *me* I yelled bloody murder. After the first year my insides felt as mushy as macaroni boiled for an hour. When I heard he was doing the job on other girls, I went to church and lit a candle."

They had all laughed but Lucy had felt her flesh twitching between her legs.

Now as she ran up the steps toward Sonny a tremendous flash of desire went through her body. On the landing Sonny grabbed her hand and pulled her down the hall into an empty bedroom. Her legs went weak as the door closed behind them. She felt Sonny's mouth on hers, his lips tasting of burnt tobacco, bitter. She opened her mouth. At that moment she felt his hand come up beneath her bridesmaid's gown, heard the rustle of material giving way, felt his large warm hand between her legs, ripping aside the satin panties to caress her vulva. She put her arms around his neck and hung there as he opened his trousers. Then he placed both hands beneath her bare buttocks and lifted her. She gave a little hop in the air so that both her legs were wrapped around his upper thighs. His tongue was in her mouth and she sucked on it. He gave a savage thrust that banged her head against the door. She felt something burning pass between her thighs. She let her right hand drop from his neck and reached down to guide him. Her hand closed around an enormous, blood-gorged pole of muscle. It pulsated in her hand like an animal and almost weeping with grateful ecstasy she pointed it into her own wet, turgid flesh. The thrust of its entering, the unbelievable pleasure made her gasp, brought her legs up almost around his neck, and then like a quiver, her body received the savage arrows of his lightning-like thrusts; innumerable, torturing; arching her pelvis higher and higher until for the first time in her life she reached a shattering climax, felt his hardness break and then the crawly flood of semen over her thighs. Slowly her legs relaxed from around his body, slid down until they reached the floor. They leaned against each other, out of breath.

It might have been going on for some time but now they could hear the soft knocking on the door. Sonny quickly buttoned his trousers, meanwhile blocking the door so that it could not be opened. Lucy frantically smoothed down her pink gown, her eyes flickering, but the thing that had given her so much pleasure was hidden inside sober black cloth. Then they heard Tom Hagen's voice, very low, "Sonny, you in there?"

Sonny sighed with relief. He winked at Lucy. "Yeah, Tom, what is it?"

Hagen's voice, still low, said, "The Don wants you in his office. Now."

This vibrant, animalistic scene is unusual not only for the verticality of the happening, but also because it is one of the few sex scenes in fiction where the size of the genitalia of *both* participants is given to the reader.

In James Dickey's blockbuster of a novel, *Deliverance*, published in 1970, there is a quick scene between the narrator and his wife before he sets off on a hairy canoe adventure down a dangerous Georgia river.

"I wish you didn't have to go off like this. I mean, didn't *want* to. I wish there was something I could do."

"There is."

"Have we got time?"

"We'll make time. There's nothing Lewis has to offer that matters all that much. He can wait. I don't feel like I can."

We lay entangled like lovers.

"Lie on your back," she said.

She had great hands; they knew me. There was something about the residue of the nursing in her that turned me on: the practical approach to sex, the very deliberate and frank actions that give pleasure to people. The blood in me fell and began to rise in the dark, moving with her hands and the slight cracking of the lubricant. Martha put a pillow in the middle of the bed, threw back the covers with a windy motion and turned face down on the pillow. I knelt and entered her, and her buttocks rose and fell. "Oh," she said. "Oh yes."

It was the heat of another person around me, the moving heat, that brought the image up. The girl from the studio threw back her hair and clasped her breast, and in the center of Martha's heaving and expertly working back, the gold eye shone, not with the practicality of sex, so necessary to its survival, but the promise of it that promised other things, another life, deliverance.

Much later in this novel, Dickey gives us a grotesque and shocking scene which was sex motivated, but hardly sexy. (See the chapter "Somewhat Bizarre.")

Nora Roberts once was quoted as saying:

"I want to die at age 120 at my keyboard after having great sex."

She is associated in many people's minds with romance novels, but she is very capable of writing hard-hitting stories like her novel, *Montana Sky*, in which this quickie scene is presented:

Reaching over, she picked up the package she'd put on the desk. "Merry Christmas, Nate."

"You got me a present?" he narrowed his eyes at the package, expecting a slam.

"Just a little one. You've been a good friend, and counselor." She smiled over the last word. "Do you want to open it now, or wait till Christmas morning?" She touched her tongue to her top lip, and all the blood drained out of his brain into his lap. "I can come back."

"I'm a sucker for presents," he told her, and ripped the paper off. When he saw the book he teetered between being faintly embarrassed and gently moved. "I'm a sucker for Keats, too," he murmured.

"So I hear. I thought when you read it, you might think of me."

He lifted his eyes to hers. "I manage to think of you without visual aids."

"Do you?" She inched closer, leaning down so that she could take hold of his loosened tie. "And what do you think?"

"I think, at the moment, you're trying to seduce me."

"You're so quick, so smart." She laughed and slid into his lap. "And so right." One quick tug on the tie and she had his mouth on hers.

Like the house, like the man, the hunger was simple and without pretense. His hands closed over her breasts, the warm, full weight of them. And when she shifted to straddle him, his hands moved around to cup her bottom.

She had already tossed his tie aside and was working on his shirt before he'd taken the first breath.

"If I'd had to go another week without your hands on me, I'd have screamed." She fastened her teeth low on his neck. "I'd rather scream with them on me."

He still hadn't managed to breathe, but his hands were busy enough, pushing that short, snug skirt of the dress up her hips, finding the delight of firm bare skin over the lacy tops of stockings. "We can't—here." He went back to her breasts, unable to decide where he needed to touch first. "Upstairs," he managed as he savaged her mouth. "I'll take you upstairs."

"Here." She threw back her head as his lips ran down her throat. He had a wonderful mouth. She'd been sure of it. "Right here, right now." On the verge of exploding already, she dragged at his belt. "Hurry. The first time fast. We'll worry about finesse later."

He was with her there. Hard as steel, aching, desperate. He struggled with the zipper in the back of her dress as she struggled with his. "I haven't got any...Christ, you're built." He dragged the dress down far enough to find those lovely, full breasts spilling over the top of a low-cut black bra. He nipped the bra down with his teeth, then used them on her.

It was a shock. She'd always considered herself healthily sexual. But when that busy mouth on her flesh shot her over the edge without a net, her body bucked, her mind spun. "God. Oh, my God." Letting her head fall back, she absorbed that first, delightful orgasm. "More. Now."

She'd exploded over him—wildly, gorgeously—and dazed him. With his hands full of her, he pressed his lips to hers and tried to think. "We have to go upstairs, Tess. I don't generally have sex at my desk. I'm not prepared for it."

"That's okay." She let her brow rest against his, drew three deep breaths. Lord, she was quaking like a schoolgirl. "I am."

Reaching back, she fumbled over the surface of the desk, knocking a number of things to the floor as he took advantage of the thrust of her breast and suckled. She heard her breath wheeze, swore she could feel her eyes cross as she groped behind her for her bag. She opened it, tossed it aside, and let a trail of condoms spill out.

He blinked. A quick guess told him there were at least a dozen. So Nate cleared his throat. "I don't know whether to be afraid or flattered."

It made her laugh. Sitting there, half naked and aroused to hell and back, she let loose a low, rocking laugh. "Consider it a challenge."

"Good call." But when he reached for them, she drew them teasingly out of reach.

"Oh, no. Allow me."

With her eyes on his, she ripped a packet off, tore it open. Mozart continued to play with grace and dignity as she freed Nate from his slacks, gave a feline hum of anticipation, and slowly, torturously protected them both.

Jane Smiley was awarded the Pulitzer Prize for her novel *A Thousand Acres*, from which this scene is taken:

I lay awake in the hot darkness, naked and covered by the sheet. Every so often, I lifted the sheet and looked under it, at my blue-white skin, my breasts, with their dark nipples, the foreshortened, rounded triangles of my legs, my jutting feet. I looked at myself while I thought about having sex with Jess Clark and I could feel my flesh turn electric at these thoughts, could feel sensation gather at my nipples, could feel my vagina relax and open, could feel my lips and my fingertips now sensitive enough to know their own shapes. When I turned on my side and my breasts swarm together and I flicked the sheet for a bit of air, I saw only myself turning, my same old shape moving in the same old way. I turned onto my stomach so that I wouldn't be able to look, so that I could bury my face in the black pillow. It wasn't like me to think such thoughts, and though they drew me, they repelled me too. I began to drift off, maybe to escape what I couldn't stop thinking about.

Ty, who was asleep, rolled over and put his hand on my shoulder, then ran it down my back, so slowly that my back seemed about as long and humped as a sow's, running in a smooth arc from my rooting, low-slung head to my little stumpy tail. I woke up with a start and remembered the baby pigs. Ty was very close to me. It was still hot, and he was pressing his erection into my leg. Normally I hated waking in the night with him so close to me, but my earlier fantasies must have primed me, because the very sense of it there, a combination of feeling its insistent pressure and imaging its smooth heavy shape, doused me like a hot wave, and instantly I was breathless. I put my hand around it and turned toward it, then took my hand off it and pulled the curve of his ass toward me. But for once I couldn't stand not touching it, knowing it was there but not holding it in my hand. Ty woke up. I was panting, and he was on me in a moment. It was something: It was deeply exciting and simultaneously not enough. The part of me that was still a sow longed to wallow, to press my skin against his and be engulfed. Ty whispered, "Don't open your eyes," and I did not. Nothing would wake me from this unaccustomed dream of my body faster than opening my eyes.

Afterward, when we did open our eyes and were ourselves again, I saw that it was only ten-fifteen. I moved away, to the cooler edge of the bed. Ty said, "I liked that. That was nice," and he put his hand affectionately on my hip without actually looking at me.

In her wonderful, 2004 serious novel, *Old Filth*, Jane Gardam, the English novelist, has a lovely, light episode involving her protagonist, Sir Edward Feathers, and his first real sexual encounter. As a nineteen-year-old officer during the end of World War II, Eddie is assigned to be in charge of guarding the Old Queen Mary who has been moved to the country for her safety. The king's mother takes a great liking to the quiet, handsome young man and is appalled to learn that he has never been to

London. She makes out a long list of museums, palaces, and historical sites for him to visit in their upcoming one-day visit to London. When the train arrives at Paddington Station early in the morning, Eddie goes directly to the address of the flat where Isobel, sister of his best friend, lives. He has longed for her for years, but this is their first encounter and his first meaningful experience with a woman.

     She put out the cigarette on the hall table ashtray, caught sight of herself in the mirror and said, "Oh my God! I forgot to comb my hair." She turned to him and grinned and it was as if the sun had come out. The sloped cat's eyes were alive again. Her long arms went up behind her head to gather up her hair into a bundle and she pinned it there. A piece of it fell down, a lion-coloured tress. Slowly, she pinned it back again, her fingers long, and lovely, and her fingernails painted the most unflinching vermilion. The dressing-gown fell open when she dropped her hands and stretched them out to him.

     "Oh Eddie. You are golden brown like a field of corn."

     Her fingertips were at his collar. When he took off his British warm, then his officer's jacket, he saw that she had loosened and then removed his tie. She draped it over a wall-light and then was in his arms.

     On the kitchen floor, naked, he thought the taxi must still be outside. He had got out of it only a minute ago. Then he forgot all that; where he had come from, where in the world he had landed, which was upon a kitchen floor, the filthy lino torn and stuck up with some sort of thick paper tape. There was an old fridge on tall legs. It was gas. Lying on the floor beside her, then above her, he could see the fridge's blue flame. It must be the oldest fridge in the world—oh, my God, Isobel. Isobel.

     Later, oh much, much later, they rolled apart.

     "I don't like this lino," he said. "It's disgusting."

     "You're spoiled. Living in palaces."

     "I was not living in palaces when you last saw me."

     "You were hardly living at all."

     They had moved on to a tiny sitting-room, which was in darkness. It smelled of booze and dust. They felt their way to a divan that stank of nicotine.

"Why is there no light?"

"Do we need it?"

"Oh, Isobel."

"It's blacked-out. Permanently. Convenient. We've never taken down the shutters since the Blitz."

"*We?*"

"The other girl and I."

"Is she likely to come in?" His head was on her stomach. His tongue licked her skin. She was warm and alive and smelled of sweat and spice and he went mad for her again.

Later. "Who is she?"

"No one you know. She's Bletchley Park. Like me."

"It's a man, isn't it?"

"No. No, certainly not. Shall we go upstairs?"

The bedroom was lighter. It had a sloping ceiling and the windows looked country as if there had once been fields outside. It had the feel of a country place; a cottage. So here's London.

"It is a cottage," she said. "London's full of cottages. And of villages. This bed is a country bed. We found it here."

The bed was high and made of loops of metal. Its springs creaked and groaned beneath them.

"Please never get rid of it. Keep it forever."

The hours passed. Wrapped, coiled, melded together they slept. They woke. Eddie laughed, stretched out to her again.

"You are like a jungle creature," he said. "In an undiscovered country."

"Eddie," she said at last, winding herself into the sheets. "I have something very important to say. How much time have we got? When's your train?"

"Five-fifteen."

"It's nearly five o'clock already."

He fled the bed, he ran for the stairs, he limped and hopped into scattered garments, he yelled with terror.

She laughed and laughed.

He found one shoe, but the other was gone.

"This will finish me," he said. "This will be the end of the Army for me."

What started out as a quickie turns into a long day's marathon.

But Eddie makes the train, just barely, and collapses in his cabin after his very educational day in London. Later Queen Mary summons him and says:

"Come back again and we can talk. I want to hear every single thing you've done today."

Poor Eddie—he's not a very good liar, but his career depends upon some imaginative talking about what *he didn't do that day*.

Lee Child's entertaining, tough, and likeable character, Jack Reacher, is busy most of the time avenging and righting wrongs, but he always has time for a quick bit of sex. Here, in the novel *Nothing to Love*, Reacher and the attractive police woman, Vaughan, have at it for the first time:

> Vaughan put her hand flat against his scar and then slid it around his back. She did the same with her other hand, on the other side. She hugged his waist and held the flat of her cheek against his chest. Then she raised her head and craned her neck and he bent down and kissed her. She tasted of warmth and wine and toothpaste. She smelled like soap and clean skin and delicate fragrance. Her hair was soft. Her eyes were closed. He ran his tongue along the row of unfamiliar teeth and found her tongue. He cradled her head with one hand and put the other low on her back.
>
> A long, long kiss.
>
> She came up for air.
>
> "We should do this," she said.
>
> "We are doing it," he said.
>
> "I mean, it's OK to do this."
>
> "I think so," he said again. He could feel the end of her zipper with the little finger of his right hand. The little finger of his left hand was down on the swell of her ass.
>
> "Because you're moving on," she said.
>
> "Two days," he said. "Three, max."
>
> "No complications," she said. "Not like it might be permanent."
>
> "I can't do permanent," he said.
>
> He bent and kissed her again. Moved his hand and caught the tag of her zipper and pulled it down. She was naked under the

dress. Warm, and soft, and smooth, and lithe, and fragrant. He stooped and scooped her up, one arm under her knees and the other under her shoulders. He carried her down the hallway, to where he imagined the bedrooms must be, kissing her all the way. Two doors. Two rooms. One smelled unused, one smelled like her. He carried her in and put her down and her dress slipped from her shoulders and fell. They kissed some more and her hands tore at the button on his pants. A minute later they were in her bed.

Afterwards, they ate, first the appetizer, then pork cooked with apples and spices and brown sugar and white wine. For dessert, they went back to bed.

Here is another typically brief Reacher encounter in Lee Child's novel *Running Blind*:

Reacher waited a long time in the stillness of Jodie's living room. His posture on the sofa changed from sitting to sprawling. After an hour he swiveled around and lay down. Closed his eyes. Opened them again and struggled to stay awake. Closed them again. Kept them closed. Figured he'd catch ten minutes. Figured he'd hear the elevator. Or the door. But when it came to it, he heard neither. He woke up and found her bending over him, kissing his cheek.

"Hey, Reacher," she said softly.

He pulled her to him and held her in a tight silent embrace. She hugged back, one-handed, because she was still carrying her briefcase, but hard.

"How was your day?" he asked.

"Later," she whispered.

She dropped the briefcase and he pulled her down on top of him. She struggled out of her coat and let it fall. The silk lining whispered and sighed. She was in a wool dress with a zipper all the way down the back to the base of her spine. He unzipped it slowly and felt the warmth of her body underneath. She pushed up with her elbows sharp points in his stomach. Her hands scrabbled at his shirt. He pushed the dress off her shoulders. She pulled his shirt out of his waistband. Tore at his belt.

She stood up and her dress fell to the floor. She held out her hand and he took it and she led him to the bedroom. They stumbled out of their clothes as they walked. Made it to the bed. It was white and cool. Neon glow from the city outside lit it in random patterns.

She pushed him down, with her hands on his shoulders. She was strong, like a gymnast. Urgent and energetic and lithe on top of him. He was lost. They finished filmed in sweat in a tangle of sheets.

And so it goes, as Vonnegut might say.

Elmore Leonard's lean prose and realistic dialogue extends even to his sex scenes, which are always explicit but never clinical or embarrassing. The following is a typical scene from his 1982 novel *Cat Chaser*. The protagonist has met a girl in the bar and invites her up to his room.

He caught the scent of her perfume, moved a cautious step and felt her hair brush his face. She was between his arms and he closed them around her now, feeling her hands slide up over his ribs.

He said in almost a whisper, "You find the candle?"

"No. It must be in the bathroom."

He said, "Do we need it?"

He felt her hands, her breath—this slim girl, not as tall as he'd remembered her, the image of her across a room. He felt the silky material covering her bare skin, the skin smoothly taut, her body delicate but firm pressing into him, their mouths brushing, finding the right place again, and this time drifting into a dreamlike kind of consciousness, Moran aware but not seeing himself, Mary moving against him, moving him, guiding gently, and Moran knew where they were going, feeling the foot of the bed against his leg and it was all the bearings he needed. They bailed out in the dark and fell into the double bed in the excitement of each other. She said, "You don't know how long..." He said, "I know." Barely moving their mouths apart to speak. She said, "God, I want you." He said, "How do you get this off?" He said, "Shit, I tore it." She said, "I don't care, tear it," pulling his belt apart. He said, "Can you wait just a second?" She said, "No." He said, "I can't either. Jesus." She said, "Don't talk." He said, "One second..." and got on his knees and pulled off her sandals and slacks and somehow got out of his pants, pausing then, catching his breath to pull his shirt over his head and when he sank down again into the bed they were naked, with nothing to make them hold back all that longing they could now release. The lights came on as they were making love, a soft bedroom glow that was just enough and could have been cued as Moran said, "Oh, man," and had to smile as he saw Mary smiling. Now they could see each other and it wasn't simply an act of their bodies, they were identified to each other, finally where they wanted to be more than anywhere. Moran's urge raised him stiffarmed, raised his face to the headboard, to the wall above them and he groaned, letting go that was like, "Gaiiiyaaa!" and brought Mary's eyes open, but she closed them again, murmuring, moving, and remained in iridescent sparkling dark as he came back to her again, winding down, settling.

She felt moisture on his back, his shoulders. She said, "Oh, God," as though it might be her last breath. Then opened her eyes to study his face in repose, his eyelashes, his eyelids lightly closed.

She said quietly, "Well...how have you been?"

It's a lovely line, considering they've barely spoken since they met. Notice how sensual and tactile this scene is, appealing to all our senses in order to put the reader into the act, into that bed:

The scent of her perfume...felt her hair brush his face...feeling her hands slide over his ribs...felt her hands, her breath...the silky material...

Considering this writing technique, here's some advice from the romance writer Marilyn Lowery. People are inclined to dismiss romance novels, but in fact writing them requires a great deal of discipline and skill, and Lowery has words in her book *How to Write Romance Novels* which one could apply to any kind of writing:

In describing the heroine's feelings, constantly remind yourself to appeal to the five senses. As the heroine tastes the food, the reader tastes the food. As the heroine feels the gorgeous brocades and velvets, so does the reader. Strange sounds attract, or sights astound. The more often you appeal to the senses, the more believable your story will be.

A good practice for such description is to actually use your own senses and write about the experience.

1. *Taste.* Try a lemon. What is the taste? How does it feel in your mouth? What is your tongue doing as you taste it? What is your mouth doing? Now try a persimmon. What is the taste? Astringent? Sweet? Add another sense. How does it *feel* on your tongue? Slippery? Slithery? How does your tongue feel after you have swallowed the bite of persimmon?

2. *Touch.* Describe the feel of a smooth piece of wood, of a rough eraser, of a strand of your hair. But do not take the easy adjectives. Have you written anything out of the ordinary?

3. *Sight.* In her poem "Aubade," Edith Sitwell says that the "morning light creaks." Light cannot creak. And yet we instinctively know what creaking light looks like. The sensation produced in one modality or point (in this case sound) when another has been stimulated (sight) is called *synesthesia.* Such a surprise can heighten your effect.

4. *Hearing.* Close your eyes and listen to the sounds around you. Alliteration can be an effective way to describe them. This technique is the repetition of a consonant sound such as, "She listened to the soft slapping of the waves on the shore."

Henry Thoreau in *A Week on the Concord and Merrimack Rivers* describes sounds of dogs barking at night, "from the loudest and hoarsest bark to the faintest aerial palpitation under the eaves of heaven." He describes the bark of the terrier, "at first loud and rapid, then faint and slow, to be imitated only in a whisper; wow-wow-wow-wow-wo-wo-w-w." Here he has used *onomatopoeia,* suiting the sound to the meaning.

Can your reader hear the rustle of your heroine's gown or the tapping of her heels on the pavement? Do you prove that your characters exist through the sounds they make or the sounds they hear around them?

5. *Smell.* Don't reserve the use of this sense for food. A man's shaving lotions smells—tell how it smells. Hair has an odor. Skin has an odor. The smell of the hero to the heroine can be powerful in a love scene. Make the scene more potent. Tell us about the *taste* of his mouth on hers. Appeal to more than one sense at a time.

Sense impressions are vital in conveying subtle love scenes. The explicit in sex can be avoided if the senses are aroused—several at once. You want your scene to be both passionate and lifelike.

9

In Flagrante Delicto

"Who you gonna believe, me or your lying eyes?"
Richard Pryor
(upon being caught in flagrante delicto *by his wife)*

Literally: While the crime is blazing—the basic situation has been a staple in literature and the theater for hundreds of years. Adultery has been around since—well—since adults.

Often it takes the form of farce: the husband goes off to work and the lover slips out of the closet and into milady's bed—but, oh dear, the husband remembers and comes back for his briefcase, and...

I like the old story of the illicit couple who are in bed making love when they hear the front door bang open, "My God, it's my husband!" she whispers. "He's probably got a pistol!"

"Where is your back door?" asks the lover in a panic.

"We don't have one!" she says.

"Where would you *like* one?" asks the lover.

So while adultery has often been treated farcically, it has an almost equal history of serious drama (think *Othello, the Iliad*, et alios).

John Updike treats the almost *in flagrante delicto* scene in his suburban novel, *Couples*, semi-seriously. The lovers, Piet and Foxy, are upstairs in a bathroom while their spouses are downstairs at the party.

They listened for steps on the stairs; there were none. Music below, and the television monologue. Her mouth opened and her tongue, red as sturgeon, touched her upper lips as she reached behind her to undo snaps. Her gown and bra peeled down in a piece. Fruit.

"Oh, God."

She blushed in answer. "I feel so gross."

"So veiny and full. So hard at the tops, here."

"Don't get them started. I must go home in an hour."

"And nurse."

"Yes. What funny sad lines you're getting here, and here. Don't frown, Piet. And gray hairs. They're new."

"Nurse me."

"Oh darling. No."

"Nurse me."

She covered one breast, alarmed, but he had knelt, and his broad mouth fastened on the other. The thick slow flow was at first suck sickeningly sweet. The bright bathroom light burned on his eyelids and seemed to dye his insides a deep flowing rose, down to the pained points of his knees on the icy tile. Foxy's hand lightly cupped the curve of the back of his skull and now guided him closer into the flood of her, now warned by touching his ear that he was giving her pain. He opened his eyes; the nipple of her other breast jutted cherry-red between ivory fingers curled in protection; he closed his eyes. Pulses of stolen food scoured his tongue, his gums; she toyed with his hair, he caressed her clothed buttocks. She was near drowning him in rose.

Knocks struck rocklike at the unlocked door inches behind them. Harsh light flooded him. He saw Foxy's free hand, ringed, grope and cup the sympathetic lactation of the breast jutting un-mouthed. She called out, as musically as before, "One moment, please."

Angela's lucid polite voice answered, "Oops, sorry, Foxy. Take your time."

"All ri-ight," Foxy sang back, giving Piet a frantic look of interrogation. Her bare breasts giant circles. A Christian slave stripped to be tortured.

His body thundered with fear. His hands were jerking like puppets on strings but his brain took perspective from the well-lit room in which he was trapped. There was no other door. The shower curtain was translucent glass, two sliding panels; his shape would show. There was a little window. Its sill came up to his chest. Realizing the raising of the sash would make noise, he motioned Foxy to flush the toilet. As she bent to touch the silver handle the shape of her breasts changed, hanging forward, long-tipped udders dripping cloudy drops. He undid the brash catch and shoved up the sash as the water closet again, feebly, drained. Setting one black dancing slipper on the lip of the tub, he hoisted himself into the black square of air headfirst. Trees on this side of the house, elms, but none near enough to grasp. His hands could touch only vertical wood and freezing air pricked by stars. Too late he knew he should have gone feet first; he must drop. This the shady rural side of the house. Soft grass. The toilet had quieted and left no noise to cover the sounds of his scrambling as he changed position. Foxy thought to turn both faucets on full. By logic she must next open the door to Angela. Piet backed out of the window. Foxy was standing by the roaring faucets staring at him and mopping herself with a purple washcloth and resecuring the bodice of her silver gown. He imagined she smiled. No time to think about it. He stood on the slick tub lip and got a leg through the little window and doing a kind of handstand on the radiator cover maneuvered the other leg through also. Button. Caught. Ah. There. He slid out on his chest and dangled his weight by his hands along Thorne's undulate shingles. Loose nails, might catch on a nostril, tear his face like a fish being reamed. Air dangled under his shoes. Ten feet. Eleven, twelve. Old houses, high ceilings. Something feathery brushed his fingers gripping the sill inside the bathroom. Foxy begging him not to dare it? Angela saying it was all right, she knew? Too late. Fall. No apologies. Pushing off lightly from the wall with his slippers and trying to coil himself loosely against the shock, he let go. Falling was first a hum, then concussion: a harpstring in reverse. His heels hit the frost-baked turf; he took a somersault backwards and worried about grass stains on his tuxedo before he thought to praise God for breaking no bones. Above him, a pink face vanished and a golden window whispered shut. They were safe. He was sitting on the brittle grass, his feet in their papery clippers stinging.

The silhouette of the trunk of the elm nearest him wavered; a female voice giggled. "Piet, you're such a show-off," Bea Guerin said.

Serious adultery is a frequent theme in the stories of Somerset Maugham. His famous novel, *The Painted Veil*, begins with this scene of *in flagrante delicto*:

She gave a startled cry.

"What's the matter?" he asked.

Notwithstanding the darkness of the shuttered room he saw her face suddenly distraught with terror.

"Someone just tried the door."

"Well, perhaps it was the amah, or one of the boys."

"They never come at this time. They know I always sleep after tiffin."

"Who else could it be?"

"Walter," she whispered, her lips trembling.

She pointed to his shoes. He tried to put them on, but his nervousness, for her alarm was affecting him, made him clumsy, and besides, they were on the tight side. With a faint gasp of impatience she gave him a shoe horn. She slipped into a kimono and in her bare feet went over to her dressing-table. Her hair was shingled and with a comb she had repaired its disorder before he had laced his second shoe. She handed him his coat.

"How shall I get out?"

"You'd better wait a bit. I'll look out and see that it's all right."

"It can't possibly be Walter. He doesn't leave the laboratory till five."

"Who is it then?"

They spoke in whispers now. She was quaking. It occurred to him that in an emergency she would lose her head and all of a sudden he felt angry with her. If it wasn't safe why the devil had she said it was? She caught her breath and put her hand on his arm. He followed the direction of her glance. They stood facing the windows that led out on[to] the verandah. They were shuttered and the shutters were bolted. They saw the white china knob of the handle slowly turn. They had heard no one walk along the verandah. It was terrifying to see that silent motion. A minute passed and there was no sound. Then with the ghastliness of the supernatural, in the same stealthy, noiseless, and horrifying manner, they saw the white china knob of the handle at the other window turn also. It was so frightening that Kitty, her nerves failing her, opened her mouth to scream but, seeing what she was going to do, he swiftly put his hand over it and her cry was smothered in his fingers.

This single, riveting, opening scene shapes the plot of the entire novel and the destinies of the characters. We don't know exactly who these people are; we're not sure even what country they are in, though the words *amah* and *tiffin* let us know that it is a foreign country. The one thing we know is that they are lovers and that they are in a very difficult situation. We would read on, we must read on. Was it really Walter at the door, and, if so, what is he going to do?

A first "encounter" between young people can be difficult and awkward enough—even without an "interruptus." The following is Stuart Dybek's account from his 2003 story "We Didn't," included in his book *I Sailed With Magellan*:

Entwined in your faded Navajo blanket, we lay soul-kissing until you wept with wanting.

We'd been kissing all day—all summer—kisses tasting of different shades of lip gloss and too many Cokes. The lake had turned hot pink, rose rapture, pearl amethyst with dusk, then washed in night black with a ruff of silver foam. Beyond a momentary horizon, silent bolts of heat lightning throbbed, perhaps setting barns on fire somewhere in Indiana. The beach that had been so crowded was deserted as if there was a curfew. Only the bodies of lovers remained, visible in lightning flashes, scattered like the fallen on a battlefield, a few of them moaning, waiting for the gulls to pick them clean.

On my fingers your slick scent mixed with the coconut musk of the suntan lotion we'd repeatedly smeared over each other's bodies. When your bikini top fell away, my hands caught your breasts, memorizing their delicate weight, my palms cupped as if bringing water to parched lips.

Along the Gold Coast, high-rises began to glow, window added to window, against the dark. In every lighted bedroom, couples home from work were stripping off their business suits, falling to the bed, and doing it. They did it before mirrors and pressed against the glass in streaming shower stalls; they did it against walls and on the furniture in ways that required previously unimagined gymnastics, which they invented on the spot. They did it in honor of man and woman, in honor of beast, in honor of God. They did it because they'd been released, because they were home free, alive, and private, because they couldn't wait any longer, couldn't wait for the appointed hour, for the right time or temperature, couldn't wait for the future, for Messiahs, for peace on earth and justice for all. They did it because of the bomb, because of pollution, because of the Four Horsemen of the Apocalypse, because extinction might be just a blink away. They did it because it was Friday night. It was Friday night and somewhere delirious music was playing—flutter-tongued flutes, muted trumpets meowing like cats in heat, feverish plunking and twanging, tom-toms, congas, and gongs all pounding the same pulse beat.

I stripped your bikini bottom down the skinny rails of your legs, and you tugged my swimsuit past my tan. Swimsuits at our ankles, we kicked like swimmers to free our legs, almost expecting a tide to wash over us the way the tide rushes in on Burt Lancaster and Deborah Kerr in *From Here to Eternity* —a love scene so famous that although neither of us had seen the movie, our bodies assumed the exact position of movie stars on the sand and you whispered to me softly, "I'm afraid of getting pregnant," and I whispered back, "Don't worry, I have protection," then, still kissing you, felt for my discarded cutoffs and the wallet in which for the last several months I had carried a Trojan as if it was a talisman. Still kissing, I tore its flattened, dried-out wrapper, and it sprang through my fingers like a spring from a clock and dropped to the sand between our legs. My hands were shaking. In a panic, I groped for it, found it, tried to dust it off, tried as Burt Lancaster never had to, to slip it on without breaking the mood, felt the grains of sand inside it, a throb of lightning, and the Great Lake behind us became, for all practical purposes, the Pacific, and your skin tasted of salt and to the insistent question that my hips were asking your body answered yes, young thighs opened like wings from my waist as we surfaced panting from a kiss that left you pleading *Oh, Christ yes*, a yes gasped sharply as a cry of pain so that for a moment I thought that we were already doing it and that somehow I had missed the instant when I entered you, entered you in the bloodless way in which a young man discards his own virginity, entered you as if passing through a gateway into the rest of my life, into a life as I wanted it to be lived *yes* but Oh then I realized that we were still floundering unconnected in the slick between us and there was sand in the Trojan as we slammed together still feeling for that perfect fit, still in the *Here* groping for an *Eternity* that was only a fine adjustment away, just a millimeter to the left or a fraction of an inch farther south though with all the adjusting the sandy Trojan was slipping off and then it was gone but yes you kept repeating although your head was shaking *no-not-quite-almost* and our hearts were going like mad and you said, *Yes. Yes wait...Stop!*

"What?" I asked, still futilely thrusting as if I hadn't quite heard you.

"Oh. God!" You gasped, pushing yourself up. "What's coming?"

"Gin, what's the matter?" I asked, confused, and then the beam of a spotlight swept over us and I glanced into its blinding eye.

All around us lights were coming, speeding across the sand. Blinking blindness away, I rolled from your body to my knees, feeling utterly defenseless in the way that only nakedness can leave one feeling. Headlights bounded toward us, spotlights crisscrossing, blue dome lights revolving as squad cars converged. I could see other lovers, caught in the beams, fleeing bare-assed through the litter of garbage that daytime hordes had left behind and that night had deceptively concealed. You were crying, clutching the Navajo blanket to your breasts with one hand and clawing for your bikini with the other, and I was trying to calm your terror with reassuring phrases such as "Holy shit! I don't fucking believe this!"

Swerving and fishtailing in the sand, police calls pouring from their radios, the squad cars were on us, and then they were by us while we struggled to pull on our clothes.

Graham Greene creates a similar situation in his fine novel *The End of the Affair*. However, it is written with much taste and economy and tension.

The writer Maurice Bendrix and the beautiful Sarah Miles have fallen deeply in love. He goes to her home and finds Henry, his friend and her husband, in bed with a cold. During the subsequent tryst, the two lovers cast caution to the wind:

There was never any question in those days of who wanted whom—we were together in desire. Henry had his tray, sitting up against two pillows in his green woolen dressing-gown, and in the room below, on the hardwood floor, with a single cushion for support and the door ajar, we made love. When the moment came, I had to put my hand gently over her mouth to deaden that strange and angry cry of abandonment, for fear Henry should hear it overhead.

To think I had intended just to pick her brain. I crouched on the floor beside her head and watched and watched, as though I might never see this again—the brown indeterminate-coloured hair like a pool of liquor on the parquet, the sweat on her forehead, the heavy breathing as though she had run a race and now like a young athlete lay in the exhaustion of victory.

And then the stair squeaked. For a moment we neither of us moved. The sandwiches were stacked uneaten on the table, the glasses had not been filled. She said in a whisper, "He went downstairs." She sat in a chair and put a plate in her lap and a glass beside her.

"Suppose he heard," I said, "as he passed."

"He wouldn't have known what it was."

I must have looked incredulous, for she explained with dreary tenderness, "Poor Henry. It's never happened—not in the whole ten years," but all the same we weren't so sure of our safety; we sat there silently listening until the stair squeaked again. My voice sounded to myself cracked and false as I said rather too loudly. "I'm glad you like that scene with the onions," and Henry pushed open the door and looked in. He was carrying a hot water bottle in a grey flannel cover. "Hello, Bendrix," he whispered.

"You shouldn't have fetched that yourself," she said.

"Didn't want to disturb you."

"We were talking about the film last night."

"Hope you've got everything you want," he whispered to me. He took a look at the claret Sarah had put out for me. "Should have given him the '29," he breathed in his unidimensional voice and drifted out again, clasping the hot water bottle in its flannel cover, and again we were alone.

As in the previously mentioned Maugham story, we don't know if the cuckolded husband *knows*, so we will keep reading avidly to find out what is going to happen.

Christopher Buckley can make any situation funny, even—or, perhaps, especially—adultery. Here is the opening scene in his novel *No Way to Treat a First Lady*:

Babette Van Anka had made love to the president of the United States on eleven previous occasions, but she still couldn't resist inserting "Mr. President" into "Oh, baby, baby, baby." He had told her on the previous occasions that he did not like being called this while, as he put it, congress was in session.

Buckley then gives us a steamy two-page description of the version of "Congress in Session" which takes place in the Lincoln Bedroom down the hall from where the First Lady is sleeping. Then, interestingly, almost as an aside from the immediately preceding scene, Buckley inserts the First Lady's thoughts:

Elizabeth Tyler McMann, First Lady of the United States, lay awake in her own still-crisp sheets, looking out the window toward the Washington Monument. Being married to America's most prominent symbol of virility, she was not blind to the irony of finding herself in bed alone, staring at the nation's most prominent phallic symbol. Not much had ever been lost on Beth McMann, other than happiness.

And this is just the first chapter!

10

Oral Exam

Oral sex is like being attacked by a giant snail.
Germaine Greer

It is hard to determine precisely when oral sex became a staple in the sex scenes of many, if not most, modern stories and novels.

D. H. Lawrence hints vaguely at it in *Lady Chatterly's Lover* way back in the 1930s. John O'Hara is less vague in his 1955 best-seller *Ten North Frederick*, though he doesn't exactly spell it out:

> She was forty-one when she married Lloyd Williams, a man her own age, and it was a great surprise on their wedding night to discover how little Lloyd knew about making love. Indeed it was weeks before she finally and fully realized that with Lloyd she could never expect to have anything but the embellishments of love-making and never the ultimate love-making itself. She had known there were men like that, and she now had married one. For two years she submitted to his technique, which excited her but gave her no relief. "What's the matter with you?" he would say. "You like it, every woman does. Most women would rather." He would become angry and frustrated by her own frustration. Time was getting short for her, she knew, and she thought of leaving him, of reopening her shop, but she would have no explanation to satisfy public

or even private curiosity; he was not a drunkard, he did not beat her, he gave her a home, he was—publicly—a much better man than Jimmy Franklin had been. Then accidentally, during one of his angriest outbursts, she learned something about him that was something of a comfort without being satisfaction.

"Didn't you ever have real intercourse with a woman?"

"Sure I did," he said.

"Those whores?"

"Yes, those whores."

"Then what's the matter with me?"

"I don't know," he said.

"I'm built the same way."

"I never liked it with them."

"What didn't you like?"

"The way I did it with them."

"The regular way?"

"Yes, the regular way."

"Then why did you do anything? Why did you do it at all?"

"I had to. A man has—desires. When I had mine I went to a whore. But it wasn't what I wanted to do. What I do with you was always what I wanted to do."

"Why can't you do the same thing with me that you did with the whores? It's what I want."

"I can't help it what you want. All I can do is what I do. Once a month I'd go to a whore and get satisfaction, quick. With you I don't want to have satisfaction, not the same kind. I want you to have satisfaction. Why don't you? You won't let yourself."

"Didn't you do the same thing with the whores?"

"No, I tell you. I hated them. I respect you."

"Is that what it is? Respect?"

"You'd never find me doing that to a whore. Never."

"I don't understand it."

"Can you understand this? You and the whores are the only women I ever knew. And what I always wanted to do I do with you."

"That's almost as if you only knew two women in your whole life."

"That's what it is. I only knew two women. The other woman was all the whores, and I hated them. And I don't hate you. I love you."

"My God," she said.

"Listen, I'm not half as queer as some people. You ought to hear some of the things in court."

"I don't want to."

"Well, then you'd know."

"I don't want to know."

"You ought to hear some of those things."

"Why don't you change? Why should I be the one?"

"Listen, I'll give you some books to read. Havelock Ellis."

"Aw, books. I never read a— "

"Not novels. Scientific."

"Doctor books. I don't want doctor books. I know what I am: a woman. And you're supposed to be a man. Are you a fairy, too?"

"Like hell I am. I wouldn't be in love with you."

"What kind of love do you call this?"

"It's a kind. There's all kinds."

"Huh. Well, I'm going to sleep."

"All right."

"You were supposed to have—you were supposed to be Rudolph Valentino and Wallace Reid rolled into one."

"If you knew more you'd understand better," he said.

"I understand enough."

"No. You don't."

"There's one thing I understand and that's there's some things I don't care if I don't ever understand."

For many years, O'Hara was considered the master of American-style dialogue.

James Jones, in his posthumous novel *Whistle*, published in 1978, waxes positively gynecological about the subject of cunnilingus. (In my naïve youth I thought that was an Irish airline, but, then, I also thought *fellatio* was a sail boat on the Nile.)

Jones describes his likeable character's confusion about this unexplored activity. In this scene between the two soldiers, protagonist Strange reveals his problem:

It was not till they had had three drinks, from the illegal pint Strange bought from the driver, that Strange brought up the other thing that apparently was on his mind.

He glanced nervously at the back of the driver's head, as they moved through the streets of downtown. Then he leaned over to Landers with a conspiratorial air.

"Did you ever eat a girl's pussy?" he whispered.

At first Landers thought he was going to some elaborate extreme as means for a joke. He began to frame in his mind some sort of joke answer. Then he saw, or sort of sensed, that Strange wasn't joking. Strange was asking in deadly seriousness.

"Why do you want to know?" Landers asked in a normal tone, to buy time.

Strange made a violent braking motion with the open palm of his good hand, for softness of voice. "Don't be embarrassed, Goddamn it," he whispered. "I'm serious."

"Well, if you put it that way. Well yes. I have," Landers whispered.

"Did you like it?" Strange whispered.

"Well yes. I liked it. In fact, I loved it," Landers whispered back.

Strange was nodding to himself. Thoughtfully. "Are you good at it?"

Everything was still in whispers, kept low by Strange's constant admonition.

"Well. Well, I don't know that there's so much to being good at it. There's this girl, Martha Prentiss? Who's around the Peabody? That loves to suck cock."

"I've had her pointed out to me, but I don't know her. Never met her." Whisper.

"I picked her up. She gave me a few pointers. But, hell. All it takes is a lot of gentleness, and a very wet tongue." Whisper.

Strange nodded, but didn't answer.

"I guess you know what a clitoris is, I guess?" Landers whispered.

"Yes, damn it. I know," Strange whispered.

"Well," Landers shrugged lamely.

"Does it smell?"

"Sure. It smells. It smells good."

"Doesn't it smell fishy?"

"It smells fishy. But it's not really fishy. It smells—Do you know the word fecund?"

Strange shook his head.

"Fecund means rich. Like rich earth. Rich for growing. Rich for growing all the rich things of summer. Ripe," Landers whispered. He began to be afraid he was sounding too poetic, and stopped.

"Ripe," Strange whispered sourly. "I'll bet it smells ripe."

Their faces were hardly a foot apart, and Strange stared into Landers' eyes intensely.

"Doesn't it smell pissy?"

"Well, yeah. A little bit. But you don't mind that. At least, I don't. But that's only at first. After a little, it doesn't smell pissy."

"Doesn't it taste?"

"No. Doesn't taste at all. Has no taste whatever. Tastes like whatever you've had in your mouth before. A cigarette. Whiskey. A steak."

Strange nodded in silence, his intent eyes not budging from Landers'.

"Say, what is all this?" Landers whispered.

"Oh, there's this girl," Strange whispered with elaborate indifference. "Wants me to blow her. Keeps telling me I'll like it. Says everybody does it."

Landers grinned. "'Show me the man who doesn't eat cunt, and I'll show you the man whose wife I can steal,'" he grinned, quoting in a whisper the ancient joke. Strange did not laugh. Strange just stared at him.

"I'll tell you one thing," Landers whispered. "Too damn many of them taste like soap."

"Taste like what?"

"Soap. So many girls are so ashamed of them, and so afraid they'll smell, that they're constantly scrubbing the hell out of them. And they taste like soap."

"Aw, shit," Strange whispered, "you're a damned expert."

"No, no. I learned it all right here. Or almost all."

That may be more than one needs to know, about—er—all that stuff. It's more than Strange cares to hear, though he eventually comes around to truly appreciate the activity under discussion.

So much of the early oral sex scenes are written by men that it is refreshing to come across a female take on this special transaction. This is from Mary Gordon's 1998 novel, *Spending*:

He put his head between my legs, nuzzling at first. His beard was a little rough on the insides of my thighs. Then with his lips, then his tongue, he struck fire. I had to cry out in astonishment, in gratitude at being touched in that right place. Somehow, it always makes me grateful when a man finds the right place, maybe because when I was young so many of them kept finding the wrong place, or a series of wrong places, or no place at all. That strange feeling: gratitude and hunger. My hunger was being teased. It also felt like a punishment. I kept thinking of the word "thrum," a cross between a throb and hum. I saw a flame trying to catch; I heard it, there was something I was *after*, something I was trying to achieve, and there was always the danger that I'd miss it, I wouldn't find it, or get hold of it. The terrible moment when you're afraid you won't, you'll lose it, it won't work, you won't work, it is unworkable and you are very, very desperate. At the same time, you want to stay in this place of desperation...at the same time, you're saying to yourself, you're almost there, you're almost there, you can't possibly lose it now, keep on, keep on a bit longer, you are nearly there, I know it, don't give up, you cannot lose it. Then suddenly you're there.

When you think of the movie *Sophie's Choice*, the classic best seller and Oscar-winning film based on William Styron's novel of the late seventies, I'll wager you think of the horrendous scene where Sophie, at the gate of the Nazi concentration camp, must make the terrible decision whether to give up her little girl or little boy to the crematorium. And, you'd be right.

But then there's the marathon sex scene near the end of the novel where the virginal narrator, young Stingo, finally achieved horizontal nirvana with his adored, beyond his grasp and beyond wildest dreams, Sophie.

I'll bet you don't even remember it, so the following will provide a refresher:

> Indeed, I'm sure it was both my residual Calvinism and my clerical disguise—also that damnable church bell—which helped cause me to falter so badly when Sophie woke me. This must have been around two in the morning. It should have been that moment in my life when literally, as the saying goes, all my dreams came true, for in the half-light I realized both by feel and evidence of my sleep-blurred eyes that Sophie was naked, that she was tenderly licking the recesses of my ear, and that she was groping for my cock. Was I asleep or awake? If all this were not puzzlingly sweet enough—the simulacrum of a dream—the dream melted instantly away at the sound of her whisper: "Oh...now, Stingo darling, I want to fuck." Then I felt her tugging off my underpants.
>
> I began to kiss Sophie like a man dying of thirst and she returned my kisses, groaning, but this is all we did (or all I could do, despite her gently expert, tickling manipulation) for many minutes. It would be misleading to emphasize my malfunction, either its duration or its effect on me, although such was its completeness that I recall resolving to commit suicide if it did not soon correct itself. Yet there it remained in her fingers, a limp worm. She slid down over the surface of my belly and began to suck me. I remember once how, in the abandonment of her confession regarding Nathan, she fondly spoke of him calling her "the world's most elegant cocksucker." He may have been right; I will never forget how eagerly and how naturally she moved to demonstrate to me her appetite of her devotion, planting her knees firmly between my legs like the fine craftswoman she was, then bending down and taking into her mouth my no longer quite so shrunken little comrade, bring it swelling and jumping up by such a joyfully adroit, heedlessly noisy blend of labial and lingual rhythms that

I could feel the whole slippery-sweet union of mouth and rigid prick like an electric charge running from my scalp to the tips of my toes. "Oh, Stingo," she gasped, pausing once for breath, "don't come yet, darling." Fat chance. I would lie there and let her suck me until my hair grew thin and gray.

The varieties of sexual experience are, I suppose, so multifarious that it is an exaggeration to say that Sophie and I did that night everything it is possible to do. But I'll swear we came close, and one thing forever imprinted on my brain was our mutual inexhaustibility. I was inexhaustible because I was twenty-two, and a virgin, and was clasping in my arms at last the goddess of my unending fantasies. Sophie's lust was as boundless as my own, I'm sure, but for more complex reasons; it had to do, of course, with her good raw natural animal passion, but it was also both a plunge into carnal oblivion and a flight from memory and grief. More than that, I now see, it was a frantic and orgiastic attempt to beat back death. But at the time I was unable to perceive this, running as I was the temperature of an overheated Sherman tank, being out of my wits with excitement, and filled all night long with dumb wonder at our combined frenzy. For me, it was less an initiation than a complete, well-rounded apprenticeship, or more, and Sophie, my loving instructress, never ceased whispering encouragement into my ear. It was as if through a living tableau, in which I myself was a participant, there were being acted out all the answers to the questions with which I had half maddened myself ever since I began secretly reading marriage manuals and sweated over the pages of Havelock Ellis and other sexual savants. Yes, the female nipples did spring up like little pink semi-hard gumdrops beneath the fingers, and Sophie emboldened me to even sweeter joys by asking me to excite them with my tongue. Yes, the clitoris was really there, darling little bud; Sophie placed my fingers on it. And oh, the cunt was indeed wet and warm, wet with a saliva-slick wetness that astounded me with its heat; the stiff prick slid in and out of that incandescent tunnel more effortlessly than I had ever dreamed, and when for the first time I spurted prodigiously somewhere in her dark bottomlessness, I heard Sophie cry out against my cheek, saying that she could feel the gush. The cunt also tasted good, I discovered later, as the church bell—no longer admonitory—dropped four gongs in the night; the cunt was simul-taneously pungent and briny and I heard Sophie sigh, guiding me gently by the ears as if they were handles while I locked her there.

And then there were all those famous positions. Not the twenty-eight outlined in the handbooks, but certainly, in addition to the standard one, three or four or five. At some point Sophie, returning from the bathroom where she kept the liquor, switched on the light, and we fucked in a glow of soft copper; I was delighted to find that the "female superior" posture was every bit as pleasurable as Dr. Ellis had claimed, not so much for its anatomical advantages (though those too were fine, I thought as from below I cupped Sophie's breasts in my hands or, alternately, squeezed and stroked her bottom) as for the view it afforded me of that wide-boned Slavic face brooding above me, her eyes closed and her expression so beautifully tender and drowned and abandoned in her passion that I had to avert my gaze. "I can't stop coming," I heard her murmur, and I knew she meant it. We lay quietly together for a while, side by side, but soon without a word Sophie presented herself in such a way as to fulfill all my past fantasies in utter apotheosis. Taking her from behind while she knelt, thrusting into the cleft between those smooth white globes, I suddenly clenched my eyes shut and, I remember, thought in a weird seizure of cognition of the necessity of redefining "joy," "fulfillment," "ecstasy," even "God." Several times we stopped long enough for Sophie to drink, and for her to pour whiskey and water down my own gullet. The booze, far from numbing me, heightened the images as well as the sensations of what then bloomed into phantasmagoria... Her voice in my ear, the incomprehensible words of Polish nonetheless understood, urging me on as if in a race, urging me to some ever-receding finish line. Fucking for some reason on the gritty bone-hard floor, the reason, unclear, dim, stupid—*why*, for Christ's sake?—then abruptly dawn-ing: to view, as on a pornographic screen, our pale white entwined bodies splashing back from the lusterless mirror on the bathroom door. A kind of furious obsessed wordlessness finally—no Polish, no English, no language, only breath. *Soixante-neuf* (recommended by the doctor), where after smothering for minute after minute in her moist mossy cunt's undulant swamp, I came at last in Sophie's mouth, came in a spasm of such delayed, prolonged, exquisite intensity that I verged on a scream. Or a prayer, and my vision went blank, and I gratefully perished. Sleep then—a sleep that was beyond mere sleep. Cold-cocked. Etherized. Dead.

I think one of the best arguments for the importance of "The Sex Scene" as a vehicle for character revelation and plot advancement appears in one of the most suspenseful novels ever written. Here is the plot of one of the earliest books (1978) of the best-selling author Ken Follett—*The Eye of the Needle*:

The invasion of Europe is about to begin. It will take place in a few hours. Every effort has been made to make the Germans think that the greatest invasion in history will take place at Pas de Calais rather than Normandy. To reinforce the deception of "Operation Fortitude," the allies have amassed a huge invasion force of hundreds of planes, tanks and trucks across the Channel in England.

The only thing is that "the great army" is made up entirely of painted plyboard images, a clever *trompe l'oeil* which has totally fooled all the Germans who have viewed it from the air. (This part is totally factual.) But one German spy, Henry Faber, in England stumbles upon the truth (in Follett's novel). He manages to get photographs of the fake army. The information will change the entire course of the war if he can get it to Hitler. But how? No radio is available to him. The real invasion will take place in a matter of hours—how can he get from England to some place on the continent where he can relay his colossal discovery?

Faber is a brilliant and ruthless spy quite capable of killing to get what he wants. The Allies call him Der Nadle because of the thin needle-like dagger he kills with. And he does kill.

In a desperate attempt to get to the continent, Faber steals a fishing boat, runs into a storm, and is shipwrecked on a tiny island off of Britain. Dressed as a fisherman, he is rescued by the English couple who live there. Faber's English is perfect. Beautiful, frustrated Lucy, with a child, and married to a cold and crippled husband, is intrigued with the handsome stranger.

It is late at night that first night, and they are all in bed and presumably asleep. But Faber knows he will have to kill them, and to make his

way to the one radio and its operator on the island in the morning. The
following scene ensues:

> And she can't sleep for thinking about him.
>
> He had not told her much about himself, she realized; only
> that he was unmarried. She did not know where he had been
> born—his accent gave no clue. He had not even hinted at what
> he did for a living, though she imagined he must be a professional
> man, perhaps a dentist or a soldier. He was not dull enough to be a
> solicitor, too intelligent to be a journalist, and doctors could never
> keep their profession secret for longer than five minutes. He was
> not rich enough to be a barrister, too self-effacing to be an actor.
> She would bet on the Army.
>
> Did he live alone, she wondered? Or with his mother? Or a
> woman? What did he wear when he wasn't fishing? Did he have a
> motor car? Yes, he would; something rather unusual. He probably
> drove very fast.
>
> That thought brought back memories of David's two-seater,
> and she closed her eyes tightly to shut out the nightmare images.
> Think of something else, think of something else.
>
> She thought of Henry again, and realized—accepted—the
> truth: She wanted to make love to him.
>
> It was the kind of wish that, in her scheme of things, afflicted
> men but not women. A woman might meet a man briefly and find
> him attractive, want to get to know him better, even begin to fall in
> love with him; but she did not feel an immediate physical desire,
> not unless she was... abnormal.
>
> She told herself that this was ridiculous; that what she needed
> was to make love with her husband, not to copulate with the first
> eligible man who came along. She told herself she was not that kind.
>
> All the same, it was pleasant to speculate. David and Jo were
> fast asleep; there was nothing to stop her from getting out of bed,
> crossing the landing, entering his room, sliding into bed next to
> him...

Of course that's what happens, and the sex is beyond Lucy's expec-
tation and experience.

She did not feel the least bit guilty afterward. Just content, satisfied, replete. She had had what she so badly wanted. She lay still, eyes closed, stroking the bristly hair at the back of his neck, enjoying the rough tickling sensation on her hands.

After a while she said: "I was in such a rush..."

"It's not over yet," he told her.

She frowned in the dark. "Didn't you?..." She had been wondering.

"No, I didn't. You hardly did."

She smiled. "I beg to differ."

He turned on the light and looked at her. "We'll see."

He slipped down the bed, between her thighs, and kissed her belly. His tongue flicked in and out of her navel. It felt quite nice, she thought. His head went lower. Surely he doesn't want to kiss me *there*. He did. And he did more than kiss. His lips pulled at the soft folds of her skin. She was paralyzed by shock as his tongue began to probe in the crevices and then, as he parted her lips with his fingers, to thrust deep inside her... Finally his relentless tongue found a tiny, sensitive place, so small she had not known it existed, so sensitive that his touch was almost painful at first. She forgot her shock as she was overwhelmed by the most piercing sensation she had ever experienced. Unable to restrain herself, she moved her hips up and down, faster and faster, rubbing her slippery flesh over his mouth, his chin, his nose, his forehead, totally absorbed in her own pleasure. It built and built, feeding on itself, until she felt utterly possessed by joy and opened her mouth to scream, at which point he clapped his hand over her face. But she screamed in her throat as the climax went on and on, ending in something that felt like an explosion and left her so drained that she thought she would never, never be able to get up.

Her mind seemed to go blank for a while. She knew vaguely that he still lay between her legs, his bristly cheek against the soft inside of her thigh, his lips moving gently, affectionately.

Eventually she said, "Now I know what Lawrence means."

He lifted his head. "I don't understand."

She sighed. "I didn't realize it could be like that. It was lovely."

"*Was?*"

"Oh, God, I've no more energy..."

He changed position, kneeling astride her chest, and she realized what he wanted her to do, and for the second time she was frozen by shock; it was just too big...but suddenly she *wanted* to do it, and *needed* to take him into her mouth; she lifted her head, and her lips closed around him, and he gave a soft groan.

He held her head in his hands, moving it to and fro, moaning quietly. She looked at his face. He was staring at her, drinking in the sight of what she was doing. She wondered what she would do when he...came...and she decided she didn't care, because everything else had been so good with him that she knew she would enjoy even that.

But it didn't happen. When she thought he was to the point of losing control he stopped, moved away, lay on top of her, and entered her again. This time it was very slow, and relaxed, like the rhythm of the sea on the beach; until he put his hands under her hips and grasped the mounts of her bottom, and she looked at his face and knew that now, now he was ready to shed his self-control and lose himself in her. And that excited her more than anything, so that when he finally arched his back, his face screwed up into a mask of pain, and groaned deep in his chest, she wrapped her legs around his waist and abandoned herself to the ecstasy of it, and then, after so long, she heard the trumpets and cymbals that Lawrence had promised.

"The Needle" is a fascinating character, an anti-hero, a true villain who we watch with fascination throughout the book, wondering how someone can kill with no human feeling, except for the country he loves. These sex scenes seem to be the only glimpse into a soul which may be able to love if only for a short time.

As in so many great stories it comes down to:

CHOICE

He thinks of killing Lucy and her family—and if so he can make his Hitler contact—but the small, tiny, flicker of love in him after their long night of sex derails his ruthless nature and ends up with—well, you can get the novel at any public library. You won't put it down.

Beyond the sexuality aspect of this scene, consider how often we've been conned by a skillful writer to care for—or at least have great interest in—a character who perhaps doesn't deserve it. (Start with Mr. Dostoyevsky's *Crime and Punishment* and keep going and going up to, at least, Truman Capote's *In Cold Blood*.)

11

"What Goes Up..."

Clyde to Bonnie in the hotel room:
"I told you, I ain't no lover."
From the movie, *Bonnie and Clyde*

A MAN'S SEXUAL FAILURE HAS BEEN ALLUDED TO, OR HINTED AT, or described in detail, in fiction for many years. My first encounter with it in literature was in William Faulkner's 1931 bleak and brutal novel, *Sanctuary*, when the malodorous racketeer, Popeye, can only do the young Temple Drake with, presumably, a corn cob.

Sometimes, nothing is presumed—And it is all spelled out in James Jones' hard-hitting 1978 novel *Whistle*. The author follows four World War II soldiers who have returned to the States from the Pacific after having been wounded in various degrees. The protagonist, Strange, loves his wife Linda, and during his long stint overseas he has dreamt of being in bed with her.

That night when they first went to bed together in the chintz-covered bed, it turned into a nearly complete fiasco. Right in mid-passion, so to speak, Strange lost his hard-on and could not get it back.

Strange didn't know what was happening to him. He tried to mumble some kind of an apology. After a little while, when nothing happened, Linda Sue patted him sympathetically on the back and rolled over with her back to him and swiftly went to sleep. She had to get up early and go do the shopping for the house before going to her job at the plant.

Deeply troubled and humiliated, Strange lay awake beside her, and wondered fearfully what was happening to him. He had dreamed of this moment so long, and so many times, it seemed absolutely unbelievable that he would not be able to perform. When he thought of all the times, and of all the places—the trenches, the bomb hole shelters, the kitchen fly, out in the edge of the woods behind the encampment—that he had tossed himself off and dreamed of this moment, it was not possible that he could have failed to perform.

There were plenty of excuses. It was true she had not helped him any, but then she never had. He had always been the one to start things. Which was the way it ought to be. Only once or twice had she ever asked him to make love to her, in their whole married life. She had never been that passionate.

It was also true that the kid brother was asleep just beyond the thin wall in the next room. And that the parents were asleep in the room on the other side. But that would never have bothered Strange before. Something had happened right in the middle of it, all the excitement had gone away, and he found he was bored.

Lying in the bed, red with the humiliation, he squirmed under the covers. And thought of himself at the last of the company's Guadalcanal bivouacs, standing just inside the edge of the jungle, peering out through the screen of leaves at the sleeping tents in the moonlight, his throbbing cock in his hand, fantasizing this night with Linda Sue hot and all over him, clawing his back, shoving it up to him, groaning and gasping with her long-suppressed desires. That was not the way it had ever happened with them, but that was the way he always fantasized it. And under the covers he felt his hard-on coming back. Looking down from the pillow, he could see it slowly thrusting up the covers between his legs.

After a minute, Strange threw off the covers and grabbing a towel padded down the hall to the bathroom and locked the door and tossed himself off in the bathroom sink, fantasizing himself out there in the fantastic night jungle. After he orgasmed he cleaned it all up neatly, feeling weird, and disturbed. When he climbed back into bed, he found himself almost hating his wife for her closed-in lack of passion. He had never been able to draw her out of it. He was furiously angry with her. And he had to keep telling himself it wasn't her fault. But what had happened to him in eighteen months away, out there?

The second night was a great deal better. But then he had spent most of the day over in Cincinnati drinking beer. So he was a lot more aggressive, and less apologetic. For that matter, with all the men around the house, there was a great deal of beer always there, too. He drank a lot of that also. There was very little else for him to do, with her at work all day. Over in Cincinnati, it was as wild and high-living and open as it apparently also was in Luxor. Servicemen with money were everywhere, and a uniform—any uniform—was a ticket into the best hotel bars and the ritziest places. You didn't have to be an officer. Everybody loved you. Or said they did, as they took your money.

That night when they went to bed, he was conscious of how beery his breath smelled, but he didn't give a damn. And Linda Sue did not complain. Half drunk and with more than enough aggressiveness now, he thought suddenly that his wife smelled funny. It was as if he could smell another man on her. When he sniffed her breasts, her skin, he of course couldn't. But it made him uneasy. Anyhow, he performed. After that, he tried several times to get her to go out with him in the night, at least to a movie. She was always too tired, always said she had to get up too early to get to work. Her job seemed to have become an obsession.

They did talk some about their savings. Or rather Strange did. Linda seemed strangely passive about it. She no longer seemed so passionately desirous of a restaurant. When he suggested, just to see how she would react, that they should maybe put it all in with the family pool and go in with them on the farm, she only smiled at him, sweetly, a little sadly, and said that if that was what he wanted, it would be fine with her.

In the end he left four days early. He had never told them exactly how many days he had, that he had exactly two weeks. It was easy enough to tell them he had only ten days, and Strange could not stand the house any longer, with its constant comings and goings and the smells and agitation of meals always in preparation.

The four extra days he spent in downtown Luxor. He discovered a nonstop poker game in a third floor room at the ritzy Claridge Hotel on North Main Street, where he got himself a room and picked up four hundred dollars in the game. He spent almost all of it, drinking and running around, either at the Claridge bar or at another hotel, the Peabody, on Union Street. He avoided picking up any women, although it would have been easy. But he felt he owed it to Linda not to.

On the last day, at the very last minute, he reported back to Kilrainey General to find out what Col. Curran was going to decide about his hand. And whether that Major Hogan had been able to cook up some bad news for him.

He did not feel he had been home at all.

Jones' motivation for writing this scene is obvious; he is not self-indulging just to include an explicit sex scene. It is certainly not sexy. It is there in the novel to ram home the terrible experiences these young men have gone through and how their outlooks, personalities, and entire lives have been changed by the ravages of war.

Which brings me, vaingloriously, to my 1952 best-selling novel, *Matador*.

Like Jones, I wanted a sex-failure scene to reveal both characters' motivations and state of mind.

Pacote, Spain's greatest matador and hero, is over the hill at age thirty. He has been drinking heavily because he knows he must retire. He also has had difficulties with his young and ambitious actress girlfriend, Socorro. It is the morning of what has been announced as his very last fight in Sevilla, and she unexpectedly shows up in his hotel suite. She greets him fondly, and all starts well enough.

"How were the baths?" he asked.

She opened her mouth, let the smoke laze out, and ended by yawning and giving a half-laugh at herself. He had the idea she had been drinking. Not much. She was too smart and too vain to ever drink too much.

"Tired?" he asked.

"Well," she said smiling. "I've been up *all* day!"

God, she had such charm when she smiled. They were so different, he thought: as different as coal and snow.

"Oh, the baths were fine." She reached over to the other chair and toyed with the tassels that dangled from the epaulet of the gold costume. She was getting restless already. "It fixed my foie up perfectly."

She loved to use French words, especially in bed, and it annoyed him because he knew she had learned every word from Guilbert.

"Now I am all ready to ruin my foie again by eating too much foie and drinking too much champagne." She had a wayward eyebrow that would assert its independence while she talked and gave her a roguish look. "I have a wonderful idea! Let's take a long walk in the Parque Maria Luisa right now."

He froze. He stared at her intently as though he hadn't heard her right and his nerves started to take over, almost letting him blurt out: A walk, good Christ, are you mad? But he clenched his hands around the brass end of the bed and compressed his lips flat against his teeth. This aloneness was what killed. This always having to go it alone, no sharing. But he had to control himself. An outburst would just bring on a defensive pout and a mumble of you-never-understand. And it was foolish and childish to say, Why don't you think about me once in a while? So he smiled and forced some warmth into his voice.

"A walk, Soco?"

"Yes, wouldn't it be fun? We can come out on the Palmera, because I told Norberto and Cucú that I'd meet them at the Bi-Lindo for a drink before the—"

She turned around and her face registered distress. "Oh, darling, I forgot that you're fighting today!"

Her apology, something so rare, made him feel superior for a few seconds, and hate welled up inside him for all the times she had hurt him with her indifference.

"Paco, love, how could I have been so thoughtless?" She kissed him.

"That's all right," he said brusquely.

His tone wiped the distress mask from her face, and she turned away sullenly.

He capitulated, as he always did, loathing himself. "That's all right," he said, meaning it this time. He pretended, to her and to himself, that she hadn't really forgotten. "It would be relaxing, take my mind off this business." He made a show of looking at his watch. "But we haven't much time. We'll take a long walk tomorrow."

"But I told La Peñaranda that we'd all go out to the finca for lunch."

He nodded numbly. It didn't make any difference, really. Tomorrow was so far away it seemed as though it were another century.

He looked at his watch again, this time to see what time it was. They'd be here in twenty minutes. He could already hear the steady clop of carriages beginning down in the streets. It wasn't the occasional clop of a dray cart or of a wagon with a plodding horse and lead donkey. It was the brisk, relentless, proud clopping of the fancy carriages rolling down the Palmera from the big homes and country estates. He could hear the gay ching-ching-ching of the harness bells.

"That's twice," said Socorro. She reached way over and turned on the radio. "You must be nervous. You've looked at your watch twice."

"I'm scared. I'm always scared."

"You're scared? I never knew that."

He thought of saying: "I guess there are things you don't know about me." But he said: "My knees start to shake when I see my name on the first contracts. They don't stop until the end of the season. Thank God this is the last."

Conchita Piquer came on the radio in the middle of "Child of Fire." Socorro sang along with her, snapping her fingers in rhythm and writhing a little in the chair: *Inside my soul I have a fountain, in case your guilt should wish to drink...* It was gypsy wailing—the "deep singing" of the bronzed folk.

He sat down on the arm of her chair, and as she shook her shoulders and clapped out the time, he could see down the front of her dress. He could see the good breasts that seemed to start their soft swell almost from the collarbone. It was as though he had never seen her undressed. He hadn't had her for weeks now. It was like a glass of water when parched—before having it, there was nothing one wanted more, and after having it, there was nothing one wanted less. But he wanted her now.

"Soco..."

He slid his hand down the front of her dress and cupped one of her wonderful breasts, gently, letting it sit in his palm. He could see the pink nipple, like the eraser on a pencil, and he could feel it burgeon, feel it swell. He moved his fingers up and pushed the shoulder strap of her dress. It slipped down to her elbow. The skin was very white compared with the rest of her tanned body, showing the line where she had protected it while sun-bathing.

"Ay, Pacorro," Soco murmured, dropping her head over against his chest, watching interestedly in the big mirror as his hand took her breast again. "Such a long time."

"Now, now, *now!*" he whispered in her ear, and her breath quickened automatically. She was easily aroused, always quicker than he, and it was fun to pull this trick on her, even at a crowded cocktail party.

"Vámonos," he breathed, standing up and pulling her to her feet. "Let's go."

"Yes," she said eagerly. She ground her cigarette out in the ashtray. She stepped out of her shoes. Then she crossed her arms, and grasping the hem of her white dress, she stripped it off over her head. She had nothing on underneath, but the white where her bathing shorts had been looked like panties against her tan. He put his arms around her feeling her nakedness against him. He felt suddenly terribly in love with her, terribly close to her. After all, this was all they really had in common.

"My love..." she said. She pulled away and pranced to the rumpled bed, her breasts bobbing saucily. She sat down on it, crossed her legs primly, cocked her head, and smiled at him mockingly, challengingly.

He shed his dressing gown and walked to the other side of the bed and sat down. When he pulled her down on her back, she squirmed her legs onto the bed ecstatically.

"Darling," she murmured happily as she kissed the scar on his chest. "Such a very naughty business before a fight, such little bad things..."

The *fight!*

Good God, he'd been able to forget it for a few moments, but now he felt the cold grab down there low in his body, felt his passion ooze into nothingness, felt his masculinity melt away.

"I'd— I'd—" he began. He sat up on the edge of the bed again. Forgotten. Forgotten that even Pepe thought there was a good chance of his getting killed today.

"I was just joking," she said. "Come on, darling." She tried to pull him down on the bed again.

"Paco!"

He stood up abruptly and walked to where he had dropped his dressing gown. After he had put it on he turned around.

"You mean you've got me like this and you're going to leave me?" she exclaimed.

"I'm sorry, Socorro."

"It was your idea," she propped herself up on one arm, "and now you're going to leave me like this?"

"I'm sorry," he said guiltily. "Afterwards. But now—now I'd better save myself for the bulls."

She knew it wasn't that. She knew it was just because he wasn't able to. "Well, this is the first time this has happened," she said, flopping back on the bed.

"Socorro, I..."

He came back and lay on the bed beside her, but she rolled away from him, giving him her back. When he started to run his hand over her body, she pulled away and got up. She put on her dress and shoes. Then she turned the radio up louder.

"Don't be angry," he said, getting off the bed. "Can't you understand that I..."

"Who's angry?" she said with an indifferent laugh. "I'm not angry. I understand how it is on a day like today."

"You know I love you very much."

She lit a cigarette; then she said: "And I love you, too."

He snapped the radio off.

"Listen," he said, and it came out now by itself, with no pre-thought. "Listen, why don't we get married?"

She looked at him with a half-smile. "How sweet of you, Paquito. If you had asked me two years ago, you never can tell, I might have jumped at the chance." She turned the radio on again, and said "Sa-sa-sa-saa," encouraging the singer.

"I didn't feel it was the life for a woman," he mumbled. What he almost admitted to himself was that he hadn't because he didn't want to marry a woman, no matter how much he loved her, that he wasn't sure he could trust. Not knowing whether she loved him or just the Pacote legend and aura and money.

But God, how he loved her, and now he felt an urgency, that he must marry her, or she would slip from him forever, that everything would slip from him. *That everything would slip from him!*

At the end of the scene, there erupts a vicious quarrel, and they break up—forever.

I think the scene works to reveal the girl's shallowness, as well as to show how the great hero has slipped, and warns the reader of what might happen in the upcoming bullfight.

(Just incidentally—very incidentally, of all the thousands of sentences I have written over the decades, none has seemed to be so memorable as my one little reference to Socorro's breast in that scene. As recently as last month, a man came up to me at a cocktail party and with mock anger said: "Damn you, ever since your book I've never looked at either a pencil or a nipple in quite the same way!")

The scene where a very young man fails sexually during his first visit to a prostitute is a familiar one in literature. Here is Cabrera Infantes' encounter in his 1979 story from *Infantes Inferno*.

Everything seemed to happen at once, and while Franqui spoke to the matron—a word which had degenerated in Havana from the dictionary's "noble and generous mother" to madam of a brothel—I was watching the show, my eyes all pupils. Never had I seen so many women together in the altogether except on the distant stage of the Shanghai or in my wildest erotic fantasies, and all of them ready for what so many refused: the gay science of screwing. Nevertheless, from amid my fascination I could hear Franqui saying something sounding like it's the first time and the stabat matron answering you can count on me, but I can't swear that was the exact exchange because I only had ears for the sumptuous sound of women crossing the salon to the beat of a mambo from the variegated Victrola, a light-and-sound sideshow, but a beacon in this whoredom by the sea. Now the madam addressed me, I mean us—I had forgotten about Pepito with all that flesh around—and shouted for somebody called Mireya, a name which has remained in my ears as very whoresome. She came over to us before big mother could add: "And Xiomara," another whorish name from then on. "Take good care of the boys," she ordered, pointing to Pepito and me, though there was no need for that index finger: One could see that all the other clients in the den of dames were bona-fide men.

Pepito chose Mireya, or rather Mireya chose Pepito, and I remained with Xiomara. I could have chosen another of those evidently ladies-in-waiting, scattered throughout the room. But I liked Xiomara of Xanadu, with her shapely body everywhere, hips, tits, and thighs: pleasure domes. Perhaps the exoticism of her name now forces the romantic association—I was already a young man of letters. Besides, her face, though not pretty, could not be called ugly, framed by her bleached-blond hair, and something about her—features, expression, walk?—made her seem (later I realized she only seemed) very young. Xiomara wore a satin slip for a dress and smiled at me as I went with her: She didn't have good teeth. We crossed the salon and went, or rather she went—she was my guide and I limited myself to following her—to the back staircase, which led to the second floor. It was a common staircase in this kind of house in Old Havana, but I insist upon remembering it, who knows why, as a spiral staircase; perhaps it's not memory but vicious circles in my imagination. After going down the brief hallway, which seems longer to me in my mind, she opened a door to a dark room, and, when she turned on the light, became a room with an empty but not very well-made bed: Someone had been lying in it not long ago and had not bothered to make it—my mother would have objected to such balled-up sheets. From this reflection on a blank sheet I was shaken by Xiomara, who, as she entered the room, as if activated by a spring (reminding me of the instant opening of the brothel door) took off her slip and was completely naked. Though apparently more modest than the naked whore who had crossed the salon, Xiomara did not wear panties, but her nudity was visible for only a second: She turned off the light as quickly as she had gotten undressed. Nevertheless, in that flash I could see her flesh, her body that reminded me—though vertical and facing me—of the almost therapeutic vision I had had on the roof, of the naked girl lying on the bed of the Pasaje Hotel room. Xiomara the whore recovered for me, now, momentarily, that lost horizontal. But it was only a memorable moment: A moment later she, Xiomara, was in bed, professionally waiting for me to form the familiar (theoretically) mythical two-backed monster, the mission-ary position, which I had never completed, she hurrying me with her visible stare in the now not so dark room. Her attitude made it obvious that she was hurrying me to undress, which I did, as far as she was concerned, desperately slowly (I heard her decayed teeth grate), but at breakneck speed for me. You see, the bottoms of my pants always get stuck on the heels of my shoes and almost make me lose my balance, which I recover with a step or two to one side and then to the other, as if dancing a conga all by myself. I was getting closer to the moment when I would penetrate, cross the threshold of the only mystery of life we can ever know and which I had yet to unveil, leaving aside childhood's instincts, my imperfect discoveries, and later learnings that were mere scratches upon the hairy door of knowledge. I rushed into bed and climbed upon Xiomara with my habitual alpine ability (climbing, I smell her perfume; cheap pomade mixed with a vague fragrance: whore's whiff in Havana lexicon but for me the odor of desire), but upon raising myself over her, the fire I felt at first when seeing this fair hetaera naked deserted me upon covering her, and instead of bulging I was limp, powerless for the promised penetration—a promise for me, for her the wages of fucking. She struggled with me, now a dead weight, but didn't do what was necessary: not to be merely physical but pleasant, offering affection, giving love if only for sale. Thus we remained in that false coitus a few minutes, which seemed to me sojourns in eternity, she rubbing the inert me uselessly against her pubes, the two of us less lewd than the lesbian spiderwomen. She got tired of fighting the whore wars: "Well, get off," was what she finally said, an ominous order, and I obeyed. She jumped out of bed and slipped her sweating body back into her satin slip. Then she turned on the light crudely and opened the door while I was still dressing, my pants now tangled above the heels of my bare feet: She ready for the next customer, I unprepared to meet my friends.

I've spoken lightly now about what was for me a collision with failure. I had expected anything—a premature ejaculation instead of capable intercourse, or more minor mishaps—but my total incapacity to function. How, after multiple masturbations, countless erections from only speaking to Beba, oral orgasms with Lucinda, how could I be practically impotent, I, presumably powerful and potent? It was all as unreal as the atmosphere of the brothel, but both are totally tactile in my memory.

The boy feels disgraced in the eyes of his companions, and the reader feels compassion for him.

But he will get over it!

Clearly, this is not a sexy scene or even a sex scene—it is an important event in the growth of a boy on the way into some sort of maturity.

12

Somewhat Bizarre

It doesn't matter what you do in the bedroom as long as
you don't do it in the street and frighten the horses.
Mrs. Patrick Cambell

In 1956, the novel *Peyton Place* by Grace Metalious caused
a major literary earthquake. Virtually unknown today, it seemed, at the
time, everyone in America was either reading it or condemning it. It was
frequently described by people (after reading every word) as being *trash*.

Actually, it was fairly well-written and hard-hitting. It depicted the
sexual practices and stories to be found in any small town. The following
is a milder scene, from the novel, based upon an incident during a high
school dance:

> "Hurry up," she whispered, and Rodney climbed in behind
> her.
> Swiftly, she pressed down the buttons on the four doors that
> locked them, and then she collapsed into the back seat, laughing.
> "Here we are," she said. "Snug as peas in a pod."
> "Come on, Betty," whispered Rodney. "Come on."
> "No," she said petulantly, "I won't. I'm mad at you."
> "Aw, come on, Betty. Don't be like that. Kiss me."
> "No," said Betty, tossing her head. "Go get skinny Allison
> MacKenzie to kiss you. She's the one you brought to the dance."

"Don't be mad, Betty," pleaded Rodney. "I couldn't help it. I didn't want to. My father made me do it."

"Would you rather be with me?" asked Betty in a slightly mollified tone.

"*Would* I?" breathed Rodney, and it was not a question.

Betty leaned her head against his shoulder and ran one finger up and down on his coat lapel.

"Just the same," she said, "I think it was mean of you to ask Allison to the dance."

"Aw, come on, Betty. Don't be like that. Kiss me a little."

Betty lifted her head and Rodney quickly covered her mouth with his. She could kiss, thought Rodney, like no one else in the world. She didn't kiss with just her lips, but with her teeth and her tongue, and all the while she made noises deep in her throat and her fingernails dug into his shoulders.

"Oh, honey, honey," whispered Rodney, and that was all he could say before Betty's tongue went between his teeth again.

Her whole body twisted and moved when he kissed her, and when his hands found their way to her breasts, she moaned as if she were hurt. She writhed on the seat until she was lying down with only her legs and feet not touching him, and Rodney fitted his body to her without taking his mouth from hers.

"Is it up, Rod?" she panted, undulating her body under his. "Is it up good and hard?"

"Oh, yes," he whispered, almost unable to speak. "Oh, yes."

Without another word, Betty jackknifed her knees, pushed Rodney away from her, clicked the lock on the door and was outside of the car.

"Now go shove it into Allison MacKenzie," she screamed at him. "Go get the girl you brought to the dance and get rid of it with her!"

Before Rodney could catch his breath to utter one word, she had whirled and was on her way back to the gymnasium. He tried to get out of the car to run after her, but his legs were like sawdust under him, and he could only cling to the open door and curse under his breath.

"Bitch," he said hoarsely, using one of his father's favorite words. "Goddamned bitch!"

He hung onto the open car door and retched helplessly, and the sweat poured down his face.

And things get worse in the little town of Peyton Place when we get into the area of incest. Well, not *really* incest, because Lucas is only Selena's step-father:

"Don't come near me, Pa," she said, and fear and revulsion made her choke on her words.

"Still a little wildcat, ain't ya, honey?" said Lucas softly. "Ain't had a man around since I left who could tame ya. I can see that." He walked closer to her, until he was standing directly in front of her. "Be nice to me, honey," he said in the old whining voice she remembered so well. "Be good to me. It ain't like I was your real pa. There ain't nothin' wrong in you bein' good to me." He put his big hands on her shoulders. "Be nice to me, honey. It's been a long time."

Selena threw back her head and spit square in his face. "You dirty old bastard," she said, her voice furiously low. "Take your crummy hands off me."

Lucas raised one hand and wiped her spittle away. "Little wild cat, ain't ya," he said, smiling his smile. "I'll fix ya. Same's I used to fix you long ago. Comere."

And then Selena realized that she was fighting for her life. In his effort to subdue her, Lucas' hands had fastened about her throat and she began to feel the lightheadedness which comes with the lack of sufficient air.

"Little bitch," he spat as her knee came up to hit him in the groin. "I'll fix ya!"

His face was congested with blood as he reached for her again, and in the quick second before his hands could touch her, she brought the fire tongs around with both her hands and smashed them with all her strength against the side of his head.

Peyton Place had sequels and became a very popular film and then an ongoing series on television.

One of the best answers to would-be authors who moan that they "don't have time to write" is the author Betty Smith. A full-time housewife and mother, she could only find time to write one page a day. But after one year of writing, in 1944, she found she had a book. It was a lovely book and made her a fortune. It was called *A Tree Grows in Brooklyn*.

The following relates the only unusual scene in the book, when the very young protagonist, Francie, encounters a murderer and child molester upon returning from school:

Francie got home at her usual time. She opened the hall door, stared up and down the long narrow hall, saw nothing and closed the solid wood door behind her. Now the hall was darkened. She walked the short length of hall towards the stairs. As she put her foot on the first step, she saw him.

He stepped out from a small recess under the stairs that had an entrance to the cellar. He walked softly but with lunging steps. He was thin and undersized and wore a shabby dark suit with a collarless and tieless shirt. His thick bushy hair grew down on his forehead almost to his eyebrows. He had a beaked nose and his mouth was a thin crooked line. Even in the semi-darkness, Francie was aware of his wet-looking eyes. She took another step, then, as she got a better look at him, her legs turned into cement. She couldn't lift them to take the next step. Her hands clutched two banister spokes and she clung to them. What hypnotized her into being unable to move was the fact that the man was coming towards her with his lower garments opened. Francie stared at the exposed part of his body in paralyzed horror. It was wormy white contrasted with the ugly dark sallowness of his face and hands. She felt the same kind of nausea she had once felt when she saw a swarm of fat white maggots crawling over the putrid carcass of a rat. She tried to scream "mama" but her throat closed over and only air came out. It was like a horrible dream where you tried to scream but no sound came. She couldn't move! She couldn't move! Her hands hurt from gripping the banister spokes. Irrelevantly, she wondered why they didn't snap off in her tight grasp. And now he was coming towards her and she couldn't run! She couldn't run! Please God, she prayed, let some tenant come along.

At this moment, Katie was walking down the stairs quietly with the bar of yellow soap in her hand. When she came to the top of the last flight, she looked down and saw the man coming at Francie and saw that Francie was frozen to the banister spokes. Katie made no sound. Neither one saw her. She turned quietly and ran up the two flights to her flat. Her hand was steady as she took the key from under the mat and opened the door. She took precious time, not aware of what she was doing, to set the cake of yellow soap on the washtub cover. She got the gun from under the pillow, aimed it, and keeping it aimed, put it under her apron. Now her hand was trembling. She put her other hand under her apron and steadied the gun with her two hands. Holding the gun in this way, she ran down the stairs.

The murderer reached the foot of the stairs, rounded it, leaped up the two steps, and, quick as a cat, threw one arm about Francie's neck and pressed his palm to her mouth to prevent her screaming. He put his other arm around her waist and started to pull her away. He slipped and the exposed part of his body touched her bare leg. The leg jerked as though a live flame had been put to it. Her legs came out of the paralysis then and she kicked and struggled. At that, the pervert pressed his body close to hers, pinning her against the banister. He began undoing her clenched fingers, one by one. He got one hand free, forced it behind her back and leaned hard against it while he started to work on her other hand.

There was a sound. Francie looked up and saw her mother running down that last flight of stairs. Katie was running awkwardly, not balancing well on account of having both hands clutched under her apron. The man saw her. He couldn't see that she had a gun. Reluctantly, he loosed his hold and backed down the two steps keeping his wet eyes on Katie. Francie stood there, one hand still gripping the banister spoke. She couldn't get her hand opened. The man got off the steps, pressed his back to the wall and started sliding against it to the cellar door. Katie stopped, knelt on a step, pushed her apron bulge between two banister spokes, stared at the exposed part of his body and pulled the trigger.

There was a loud explosion and the smell of burnt cloth as the hole in Katie's apron smoldered. The pervert's lip curled back to show broken dirty teeth. He put both hands on his stomach and fell. His hands came away as he hit the floor and blood was all over that part of him that had been worm-white. The narrow hall was full of smoke.

The 1945 film of Smith's book was one of the first directed by Elia Kazan and it won several Oscars.

In his 1970 novel, *Mr. Sammler's Planet*, Nobel Prize and Pulitzer Prize winner Saul Bellow presents the following scene—unusual to say the least—near the beginning of the book.

Mr. Arthur Sammler, an old European gentleman, is riding a crowded uptown Manhattan bus when he notices a black pickpocket at work:

He saw that in the long rear seat he had cornered someone. Powerfully bent, the wide back concealed the victim from the other passengers. Only Sammler, because of his height, could see. Nothing to be grateful to height or vision for. The cornered man was old, was weak; poor eyes, watering with terror; white lashes, red lids, and a sea-mucus blue, his eyes, the mouth open with false teeth dropping from the upper gums. Coat and jacket were open also, the shirt pulled forward like detached green wallpaper, and the lining of the jacket ragged. The thief tugged his clothes like a doctor with a clinic patient. Pushing aside tie and scarf, he took out the wallet. His own homburg he then eased back (an animal movement, simply) slightly from his forehead, furrowed but not with anxiety. The wallet was long—leatherette, plastic. Open, it yielded a few dollar bills. There were cards. The thief put them in his palm. Read them with a tilted head. Let them drop. Examined a green federal-looking check, probably Social Security. Mr. Sammler in his goggles was troubled in focusing. Too much adrenalin was passing with light, thin, frightening rapidity through his heart. He himself was not frightened, but his heart seemed to record fear, it had a seizure. He recognized it—knew what name to apply: tachycardia. Breathing was hard. He could not fetch in enough air. He wondered whether he might not faint away. Whether worse might not happen. The check the black man put into his own pocket. Snapshots like the cards fell from his fingers. Finished, he then dropped the wallet back into the gray, worn, shattered lining, flipped back the old man's muffler. In ironic calm, thumb and forefinger took the knot of the necktie and yanked it approximately, but only approximately, into place. It was at this moment that, in a quick turn of the head, he saw Mr. Sammler. Mr. Sammler seen seeing was still in rapid currents with his heart. Like an escaping creature racing away from him. His throat ached, up to the root of the tongue. There was a pang in the bad eye. But he had some presence of mind. Gripping the overhead chrome rail, he stooped forward as if to see what street was coming up. Ninety-sixth. In other words, he avoided a gaze that might be held, or any interlocking of looks. He acknowledged nothing, and now began to work his way toward the rear exit, gently urgent, stooping doorward. He reached, found the cord, pulled, made it to the step, squeezed through the door, and stood on the sidewalk holding the umbrella by the fabric, at the button.

He had beaten the pickpocket to the door of the bus, but still he didn't feel safe. However, he knew something about lying low.

He had learned in Poland, in the war, in forests, cellars, passageways, cemeteries. Things he had passed through once which had abolished a certain margin or leeway ordinarily taken for granted. Taking for granted that one will not be shot stepping into the street, nor clubbed to death as one stoops to relieve oneself, nor hunted in an alley like a rat. This civil margin once removed, Mr. Sammler would never trust the restoration totally. He had had little occasion to practice the arts of hiding and escape in New York. But now, although his bones ached for the bed and his skull was famished for the pillow, he sat at the counter with his tea. He could not use buses any more. From now on it was the subway. The subway was an abomination.

But Mr. Sammler had not shaken the pickpocket. The man obviously could move fast. He might have forced his way out of the bus to mid-block and sprinted back, heavy but swift in homburg and camel's hair coat. Much more likely, the thief had observed him earlier, had once before shadowed him, had followed him home. Yes, that must have been the case. For when Mr. Sammler entered the lobby of his building the man came up behind him quickly, and not simply behind but pressing him bodily, belly to back. He did not lift his hands to Sammler, but pushed. There was no building employee. The doormen, also running the elevator, spent much of their time in the cellar.

"What is the matter? What do you want?" said Mr. Sammler.

He was never to hear the black man's voice. He no more spoke than a puma would. What he did was to force Sammler into a corner beside the long blackish carved table, a sort of Renaissance piece, a thing which added to the lobby melancholy, by the buckling canvas of the old wall, by the red-eyed lights of the brass double fixture. There the man held Sammler against the wall with his forearm. The umbrella fell to the floor with a sharp crack of the ferrule on the tile. It was ignored. The pickpocket unbuttoned himself. Sammler heard the zipper descend. Then the smoked glasses were removed from Sammler's face and dropped on the table. He was directed, silently, to look downward. The black man had opened his fly and taken out his penis. It was displayed to Sammler with great oval testicles, a large tan-and-purple uncircumcised thing—a tube, a snake; metallic hairs bristled at the thick base and the tip curled beyond the supporting, demonstrating hand, suggesting the fleshly mobility of an elephant's trunk, though the skin was somewhat iridescent rather than thick or rough. Over the forearm and fist that held him Sammler was required to gaze at this organ. No compulsion would have been necessary. He would in any case have looked.

The interval was long. The man's expression was not directly menacing but oddly, serenely masterful. The thing was shown with mystifying certitude. Lordliness. Then it was returned to the trousers. *Quod erat demonstrandum.* Sammler was released. The fly was closed, the coat buttoned, the marvelous streaming silk salmon necktie smoothed with a powerful hand on the powerful chest. The black eyes with a light of super candor moved softly, concluding the session, the lesson, the warning, the encounter, the transmission. He picked up Sammler's dark glasses and returned them to his nose. He then unfolded and mounted his own, circular, of gentian violet gently banded with the lovely Dior gold.

Certainly, a unique and unforgettable, though disturbing, scene.

"Is there sex after death?"—sounds like an article out of a copy of the *Readers' Digest*. But the following is William Faulkner's answer to the question in his much anthologized 1931 story "A Rose For Emily."

Faulkner, like Bellow, won the Nobel Prize and not only one Pulitzer, but two. "A Rose for Emily" is a story every would-be writer should know—and enjoy.

An eccentric woman in the South, jilted by her lover, becomes a recluse in her mansion. The author gives us a slight clue when Miss Emily buys some rat poison early in the story, but we don't have all the information until the end—the *very* end, after the old lady's funeral:

Already we knew that there was one room in that region above stairs which no one had seen in forty years, and which would have to be forced. They waited until Miss Emily was decently in the ground before they opened it.

The violence of breaking down the door seemed to fill this room with pervading dust. A thin, acrid pall as of the tomb seemed to be everywhere upon this room decked and furnished as for a bridal: upon the valence curtains of faded rose color, upon the rose-shaded lights, upon the dressing table, upon the delicate array of crystal and the man's toilet things backed with tarnished silver, silver so tarnished that the monogram was obscured. Among them lay a collar and tie, as if they had just been removed, which, lifted, left upon the surface a pale crescent in the dust. Upon a chair hung the suit, carefully folded; beneath it the two mute shoes and the discarded socks.

The man himself lay in the bed.

For a long while we just stood there, looking down at the profound and fleshless grin. The body had apparently once lain in the attitude of an embrace, but now the long sleep that outlasts love, that conquers even the grimace of love, had cuckolded him. What was left of him, rotted beneath what was left of the nightshirt, had become inextricable from the bed in which he lay; and upon him and upon the pillow beside him lay that even coating of the patient and biding dust.

Then we noticed that in the second pillow was the indentation of a head. One of us lifted something from it, and leaning forward, that faint and invisible dust dry and acrid in the nostrils, we saw a long strand of iron-gray hair.

As long as we're considering the sexual writings of Nobel Prize winners, here is a famous one by John Steinbeck (who won the Nobel Prize in 1962). This is from a short story called "The Ears of Johnny Bear."

And a good story it is.

Johnny Bear is retarded, to say the least, but he is a human recording machine; he is a Peeping Tom, going from house to house, and, without understanding what he is hearing, the conversations are implanted word-for-word, no matter in what language, in Johnny's brain. He then goes to the Buffalo Bar to recite his previous night's eavesdropping verbatim in exchange for a shot or two of whiskey.

The basic story revolves around the Hawkins' sisters, wealthy unmarried ladies. They are beloved and respected by the townspeople who consider them their aristocrats. When Miss Army, the younger of the two, hangs herself, the town is shocked. And they are even more shocked when they learn she was pregnant. They learn it from Johnny Bear, who repeats a conversation he eavesdropped between the sister and the town doctor. Then the real shocker comes when Johnny Bear repeats a conversation in Chinese between Miss Amy and the Chinese fieldhand who we learn was her lover.

Though sex is the core and pay-off of the story, we do not "see" any sex; it takes place off-camera, and we know about it only through the narration of Johnny Bear.

If Steinbeck gives us none of the details of Miss Hawkins' affair, perhaps Joyce Carol Oates gives us more details than we might need or want concerning her protagonist's Rebecca's first affair. In her wonderfully different novel *The Gravedigger's Daughter*, the eponymous young girl finally is alone in a hotel room with the love of her life, Tignor, who is older—and perhaps not too savory. He has abruptly given her a ring.

"Go on, girl. Try it. See if it fits."

Seeing that Rebecca was blinded by tears, Tignor, with his clumsy fingers, took the ring from her and tried to push it onto the third finger of her right hand. Almost, the ring fit. If he had wanted to push harder, it would fit.

Faintly Rebecca said, "It's so beautiful. Tignor, thank you..."

She was nearly overcome with emotion. Yet a part of her mind remained detached, mocking. *It's that ring. He stole it from that room. That man he almost killed. He's waiting for you to recognize it, to accuse him.*

Rebecca took the ring from Tignor and slipped it onto a smaller finger, where it fit loosely.

She kissed Tignor. She heard herself laughing gaily.

"Tignor, does this mean we're engaged?"

Tignor snorted in derision. "Hell it does, girl. What it means is I gave you a damn pretty ring, that's what it means." He was very pleased with himself.

Beyond the tall, gaunt window framed by heavy velvet drapes, the winter sun had nearly disappeared below the tree line. The snow was glowering a somber shadowy white, the myriad dog tracks that had troubled Rebecca's eye had vanished. Rebecca laughed again, the rich flamey bourbon was making her laugh. So many surprises in this room, that had gone to her head. She was short of breath as if she'd been running.

She was in Tignor's arms, and kissing him recklessly. Like one throwing herself from a height, falling, diving into water below, blindly trusting that the water would receive her and not crush her.

"Tignor! I love you. Don't leave me, Tignor..."

She spoke fiercely, she was half-sobbing. Clutching at him, the fatty-muscled flesh of his shoulders. Tignor kissed her, his mouth was unexpectedly soft. Now Rebecca had come to him, now he was startled by her passion, almost hesitant himself, holding back. Always in their lovemaking it was Rebecca who stiffened, who held back. Now she was kissing him hard, in a kind of frenzy, her eyes shut hard seeing the brilliant glittering ice on the river, blue-tinted in the sun, that hardness she wished for herself. She tightened her arms around his neck in triumph. If she was afraid of him now, his maleness, she would give no sign. If he had stolen the ring he had stolen it for her, it would be hers now. She opened her mouth to his. She would have him now, she would give herself over to him. She hated it, her soul so exposed. The man's eyes seeing her, that had seen so many other women naked. She could not bear it, such exposure, yet she would have him now. Her body, that was a woman's body now, the heavy breasts, the belly, the patch of wiry black pubic hair that trailed upward to her navel, like seaweed, that filled her with angry shame.

Like tossing a lighted match onto dried kindling, Rebecca kissing Niles Tignor in this way.

Hurriedly he pulled off their clothing. He took no care that the neck of the angora sweater was stretched and soiled, he had no more awareness of Rebecca's clothing than he had of the floral-print wallpaper surrounding them. Where he could not unbutton or unfasten, he yanked. And his own clothes, too, he would open partway, fumbling in haste. He dragged back the heavy bedspread, throwing it onto the floor, scattering the dollar bills another time, onto the carpet. Some of these bills would be lost, hidden inside the folds of the brocade bedspread, for a chambermaid to discover. He was impatient to make love to Rebecca, yet Tignor was an experienced lover of inexperienced girls, he had presence of mind enough to bring out from the bathroom not one but three towels, the very towels Rebecca had been too shy to soil with her wetted hands, and these towels he folded deftly, and lay on the opened bed, beneath Rebecca's hips.

Rebecca wondered why, why such precaution. Then she knew.

Then, somewhat later in the scene:

"Tignor! Pour me some bourbon."

This Tignor would do, happily. For Tignor too needed a drink.

Lifting the glass to Rebecca's chafed lips as she lay in the churned soiled sheets. Her hair was sticking to her sweaty face and neck, her breasts and belly were slick with sweat, her own and Tignor's. He had made her bleed, the folded towels had only just been adequate to absorb the bleeding.

Making love to her, Tignor had been heedless of her muffled cries. Moving upon her massive and obliterating as a landslide. The weight of him! The bulk, and the heat! Rebecca had never experienced anything like it. So shocked, her eyes flew open. The man pumping himself into her, as if this action were his very life, he could not control its urgency that ran through him flame-like, catastrophic. He had scarcely known her, he could not have been aware of her attempts to caress him, to kiss him, to speak his name.

Afterward, she'd tried to hide the bleeding. But Tignor saw, and whispered through his teeth. "God *damn*."

Rebecca was all right, though. If there was pain, throbbing pain, not only between her legs where she was raw, lacerated, as if he'd shoved his fist up inside her, but her backbone, and the reddened chafed skin of her breasts, and the marks of his teeth on her neck, yet she would not cry, God damn she refused to cry. She understood that Tignor was feeling some repentance. Now the flame-like urgency had passed, now he'd pumped his life into her, he was feeling a male shame, and a dread of her breaking into helpless sobs for then he must console her, and his sexual nature was not one comfortable with consolation. Guilt would madden Niles Tignor, like a horse beset by horseflies.

He hadn't *taken caution* as he called it, either. This he had certainly meant to do.

Rebecca knew, by instinct, that she must not make Tignor feel guilty, or remorseful. He would dislike her, then. He would not want to make love to her again. He would not love her, and he would not marry her.

This excerpt shows one how very important a sex scene can be to the characters and their story. In a very short time, we learn that we do not care for Mister Tignor very much, and that our girl Rebecca should un-friend him as soon as possible.

In contrast to Joyce Carol Oates' giving us all the details, we find James M. Cain, who wrote about sexual motivation in his block-busting novels such as *The Postman Always Rings Twice*, *Double Jeopardy*, and *Mildred Pierce*, but gives us very few details. He gives us just enough to make the reader fill in the salacious blanks.

In his classic hard-boiled novel, *Serenade*, Cain gives us a step-by-step account of how to kill, cook, and eat a three-foot iguana while camping in a deserted Mexican church.

"What are you doing? Let that goddam thing alone!"

When I spoke he shot out for the next rock like something on springs, but she made a swipe and caught him in mid-air. He landed about ten feet away, with his yellow belly showing and all four legs churning him around in circles. She scrambled over, hit him again, and then she grabbed him. "Machete! Quick, bring machete!"

"Machete, hell, let him go I tell you!"

"Is iguana! We cook! We eat!"

"Eat!—that thing?"

"The machete, the machete!"

Etcetera, etcetera, up to and including the delicious iguana entrée, plus how to season it, but not much do we get on the intimate transaction that took place in front of the altar before dinner, sort of a sexual hors d'oeuvre:

I got up, blew out all the candles but one, and took that one with me. I started up past the crucifix to cross over to the vestry room. She wasn't at the crucifix. She was out in front of the altar. At the foot of the crucifix I saw something funny and held the candle to see what it was. It was three eggs, in a bowl. Beside them was a bowl of coffee and a bowl of ground corn. They hadn't been there before. Did you ever hear of a Catholic putting eggs, coffee, and corn at the foot of the cross? No, and you never will. That's how an Aztec treats a god.

I crossed over, and stood behind her, where she was crouched down, on her knees, her fact touching the floor and her hands pressing down beside it. She was stark naked, except for a rebozo over her head and shoulders. There she was at last, stripped to what god put there. She had been sliding back to the jungle ever since she took off that first shoe, coming out of Taxco, and now she was right in it.

A white spot from the sacristy lamp kept moving back and forth, on her hip. A creepy feeling began to go up my back, and then my head began to pound again, like sledge hammers were inside of it. I blew out the candle, knelt down, and turned her over.

When it was over we lay there, panting. Whatever it was that she had done to me, that the rest of it had done to me, I was even. She got up and went back to the car.

James M. Cain's books, though somewhat dated, are very instructive to a writer who wants to find out about that all-important trick:

"How do you keep the reader turning the pages up till the end?"

To me, as a young writer, Cain was the most influential in that regard, even more than Hemingway.

These days, making the literary sexual scene different is not easy when one considers the preponderance of what has gone before. The late Robert B. Parker always seemed to bring a freshness to the obligatory sex scenes in each of his dozens of "Spencer For Hire" novels. Detective Spencer always seems to have time for a light-hearted romp with his longtime lady-friend, Susan, no matter how threatening the bad guys out there were.

In his 1996 novel, *Chance*, Spencer and Susan are in Las Vegas trying to find a missing woman. Susan comes in their fancy hotel room after a shopping spree. Spencer's on the phone.

"Stay put, watch Meeker. Look for Shirley."

"Better do what he says."

"Certainly," I said. "Susan and I are reviewing her shopping. I'll talk to you later."

We hung up. Susan was holding up the colorful cowboy boots.

"What do you think?" she said.

"You know," I said, "what would be a great look?"

Susan put her finger to her lips.

"I'll try them on," she said.

She took the cowboy boots and went into the bedroom. Outside the volcano began to rumble. I got up and went to the window. It would be embarrassing to go home and say I'd never seen it. I stared down at the plastic volcano as flame and smoke erupted from the top and fire ran down the sides mixing with the water which flowed from the fountain. This went on for several minutes and then stopped. And the mountain turned back into a waterfall. I stared at it for a while. Maybe it would be embarrassing to go home and say I had seen it. I turned back toward the room. Susan came into the living room with her cowboy boots on and no other clothes.

"Howdy," I said.

I'd seen her naked often. But in all the time I'd known her, I never saw her naked without a sense that if I weren't so manly I'd feel giddy. In fact I never saw her at all, dressed or undressed, without that feeling.

"Every time I buy boots you have the same suggestion as to how I should wear them," Susan said.

"Well," I said, "you can't say it's not a good suggestion."

"No," Susan said. "I can't."

"The gold necklace is a nice touch," I said.

"Thank you."

"You're welcome."

Susan's eyes narrowed slightly, and she looked at me sort of sideways as if squinting into the sun.

"You want to canter on into the bedroom," she said. "Buckaroo?"

"You sure you want to do that now?" I said. "The volcano's due to go off again in fifteen minutes."

She smiled the smile at me, the one that could launch a thousand ships and burn the topless towers of Ilium. She walked slowly toward me.

"So are you," she said.

Parker's novels always have a sex scene that is amusing, minimal, sexy, and in good taste. Not as easy a literary trick to pull off as it might sound.

The late Norman Mailer can be an unpleasant writer, an uneven writer, and an infuriating writer, but rarely is he a dull writer.

And that, of course, applies to his sex scenes, which are usually tough and graphic. The following is a musing by the protagonist of Mailer's *The Time of Our Time* (1959).

The narrator, an American young man, lives in Manhattan, and, improbably, teaches bullfighting techniques in his Greenwich Village studio.

But on this particular morning, when I turned over a little more, there was a girl propped on one elbow in the bed beside me, no great surprise, because this was the year of all the years in my life when I was scoring three and four times a week, literally combing the pussy out of my hair, which was no great feat if one knew the Village and the scientific temperament of the Greenwich Village mind. I do not want to give the false impression that I was one of the lustiest to come adventuring down the pike—I was cold, maybe by birth, certainly by environment: I grew up in a Catholic orphanage—and I had had my little kinks and cramps, difficulties enough just a few years ago, but I had passed through that, and I was going now on a kind of disinterested but developed competence; what it came down to was that I could go an hour with the average girl without destroying more of the vital substance than a good night's sleep could repair, and since that sort of stamina seems to get advertised, and I had my good looks, my blond hair, my height, build, and bullfighting school, I suppose I became one of the Village equivalents of an Eagle Scout badge for the girls. I was one of the credits needed for a diploma in the sexual humanities, I was par for a good course, and more than one of the girls and ladies would try me on an off-evening like comparison-shoppers to shop the value of their boyfriend, lover, mate, or husband against the certified professionalism of Sergius O'Shaugnessy.

Now if I make this sound bloodless, I am exaggerating a bit—even an old habit is livened once in a while with color, and there were girls I worked to get and really wanted, and nights when the bull was far from dead in me. I even had two women I saw at least once a week, each of them, but what I am trying to emphasize is that when you screw too much and nothing is at stake, you begin to feel like a saint. It was a hell of a thing to be holding a nineteen-year-old girl's ass in my hands, hefting those young kneadables of future power, while all the while the laboratory technician in my brain was deciding that the experiment was a routine success—routine because her cheeks looked and felt just about the way I had thought they would while I was sitting beside her in the bar earlier in the evening, and so I still had come no closer to understanding my scientific compulsion to verify in the retort of the bed how accurately I had predicted the form, texture, rhythm and surprise of any woman who caught my eye.

Only an ex-Catholic can achieve some of the rarer amalgams of guilt, and the saint in me deserves to be recorded. I always felt an obligation—some noblesse oblige of the kindly cocksman—to send my women away with no great wounds to their esteem, feeling at best a little better than when they came in, I wanted it to be friendly (what vanity of the saint!). I was the messiah of the one-night stand, and so I rarely acted like a pig in bed, I wasn't greedy, I didn't grind all my tastes into their mouths, I even abstained from springing too good a lay when I felt the girl was really in love with her man, and was using me only to give love the benefit of new perspective. Yes, I was a good sort...

But then:

It was to be a little different this morning, however. As I said, I turned over in my bed, and looked at the girl propped on her elbow beside me. In her eyes there was a flat hatred which gave no ground—she must have been staring like this at my back for several minutes, and when I turned, it made no difference—she continued to examine my face with no embarrassment and no delight.

Pretty tame stuff, considering it's from The Mailer.

Perhaps this next scene, an unforgettable one from James Dickey's powerful novel *Deliverance*, belongs more in the *ugh* chapter.

A group of friends, young outdoorsmen, are canoeing down a Southern river when they fall into the hands of a strange group of vicious locals. The first victim is the pudgy Bobby.

They both went toward Bobby, the lean man with the gun this time. The white-bearded one took him by the shoulders and turned him around toward downstream.

"Now let's you just drop them pants," he said.

Bobby lowered his hands hesitantly. "Drop...?" he began.

My rectum and intestines contracted. Lord God.

The toothless man put the barrels of the shotgun under Bobby's right ear and shoved a little. "Just take 'em right on off," he said.

"I mean, what's this all…" Bobby started again weakly.

"Don't say nothin'," the older man said. "Just do it."

The man with the gun gave Bobby's head a vicious shove, so quick that I thought the gun had gone off. Bobby unbuckled his belt and unbuttoned his pants. He took them off, looking around ridiculously for a place to put them.

"Them panties too," the man with the belly said.

Bobby took off his shorts like a boy undressing for the first time in a gym, and stood there plump and pink, his hairless thighs shaking, his legs close together.

"See that log? Walk over yonder."

Wincing from the feet, Bobby went slowly over to a big fallen tree and stood near it with his head bowed.

"Now git on down crost it."

The tall man followed Bobby's head down with the gun as Bobby knelt over the log.

"Pull your shirt-tail up, fat-ass."

Bobby reached back with one hand and pulled his shirt up to his lower back. I could not imagine what he was thinking.

"I said *up*," the tall man said. He took the shotgun and shoved the back of the shirt up to Bobby's neck, scraping a long red mark along his spine.

The white-bearded man was suddenly also naked up to the waist. There was no need to justify or rationalize anything; they were going to do what they wanted to. I struggled for life in the air, and Bobby's body was still and pink in an obscene posture that no one could help. The tall man restored the gun to Bobby's head, and the other one knelt behind him.

A scream hit me, and I would have thought it was mine except for the lack of breath. It was a sound of pain and outrage, and was followed by one of simple and wordless pain. Again it came out of him, higher and more carrying. I let all the breath out of myself and brought my head down to look at the river. Where are they, every vein stood out to ask, and as I looked the bushes broke a little in a place I would not have thought of and made a kind of complicated alleyway out onto the stream—I was not sure for a moment whether it was water or leaves—and Lewis' canoe was in it. He and Drew both had their paddles out of water, and then they turned and disappeared.

The white-haired man worked steadily on Bobby, every now and then getting a better grip on the ground with his knees. At last he raised his face as though to howl with all his strength into the leaves and the sky, and quivered silently while the man with the gun looked on with an odd mixture of approval and sympathy. The whorl-faced man drew back, drew out.

The standing man backed up a step and took the gun from behind Bobby's ear. Bobby let go of the log and fell to his side, both arms over his face.

We all sighed. I could get better breath, but only a little.

The two of them turned to me.

Bobby never really recovers from the attack.

William Trevor is one of the greatest writers of short stories of our time. In a lovely, dead-panned, very English story called "Lovers of Their Time," Norman and Marie fall in love, but it is confined to having drinks in the great western Royal Hotel after work. They have no place to go to consummate—and he is married. Renting a room in the hotel is out of the question, but finally:

December came. It was no longer foggy, but the weather was colder, with an icy wind. Every evening, before her train, they had their drink in the hotel. "I'd love to show you that bathroom," he said once. "Just for fun." He hadn't been pressing it in the least; it was the first time he mentioned the bathroom since he'd mentioned it originally. She giggled and said he was terrible. She said she'd miss her train if she went looking at bathrooms, but he said there'd easily be time. "Gosh!" she whispered, standing in the doorway, looking in. He put his arm around her shoulders and drew her inside, fearful in case a chambermaid should see them loitering there. He locked the door and kissed her. In almost twelve months it was their first embrace in private.

They went to the bathroom during the lunch hour on New Year's Day, and he felt it was right that they should celebrate in this way the anniversary of their first real meeting. His early impression of her, that she was of a tartish disposition, had long since been dispelled. Voluptuous she might seem to the eye, but beneath that misleading surface she was prim and proper. It was odd that Hilda, who looked dried-up and wholly uninterested in the sensual life, should also belie her appearance. "I've never done it before," Marie confessed in the bathroom, and he loved her the more for that. He loved her simplicity in this matter, her desire to remain a virgin until her wedding. But since she repeatedly swore that she could marry no one else, their anticipating of their wedding-night did not matter. "Oh, God, I love you," she whispered, naked for the first time in the bathroom. "Oh, Norman, you're so good to me."

After that it became a regular thing. He would saunter from the hotel bar, across the huge entrance lounge, and take a lift to the second floor. Five minutes later she would follow, with a towel brought specially from Reading in her handbag. In the bathroom they always whispered, and would sit together in a warm bath after their love-making, still murmuring about the future, holding hands beneath the surface of the water. No one ever rapped on the door to ask what was going on in there. No one ever questioned them as they returned, separately, to the bar, with the towel they'd shared damping her compact and her handkerchief.

Years instead of months began to go by. On the juke-box in the Drummer Boy the voice of Elvis Presley was no longer heard. "*Why she had to go I don't know,*" sang the Beatles, "*she didn't say...I believe in yesterday.*"

Here's how they thought about their bathtub trysts:

Romance ruled their brief sojourns, and love sanctified—or so they believed—the passion of their physical intimacy. Love excused their eccentricity, for only love could have found in them a willingness to engage in the deception of a hotel and the courage that went with it: that they believed most of all.

It is a very tender and rather innocent story about sex and true love.

Totally different was the 1946 blockbuster of a novel by Edmund Wilson called *Memoirs of Hecate County*.

He was considered America's greatest critic, spoke six languages, taught at Harvard and Yale, and wrote books and a very dirty novel. The book consists of six interrelated stories, one of which describes the bizarre lust the protagonist has for beautiful, aloof Imogen. She has a very bad back, wears a brace of some sort, and refuses to indulge in sex. For a long time, that is, until they finally manage to comingle. Anyway, there is a great deal of sex that is more clinical than sexy, and, in 1947, the State of New York declared the book obscene and took the publisher, Doubleday and Company, to court.

The writer and esteemed critic Lionel Trilling was called as a witness on behalf of the defendants.

> Q. Now, you testified in answer to Mr. Schilback's question that this book had literary significance, is that correct?
>
> Trilling: Yes, sir.
>
> Q. Now, I just want to read a couple of parts here and ask you if you feel that the parts that I read are necessary to assist the book in being of literary value. [Reads passage from pp. 250–251]

> I was actually embarrassed and baffled by a body which surpassed in its symmetry anything I had ever expected. I suppose that, though I had not imagined it, I had been fearing some deformity or at least defect; but, even if I had not, I should hardly have been prepared for a woman who—alone in my experience— did really resemble a Venus. She seemed perfectly developed and proportioned, with no blight from her spinal disease: she was quite straight and had the right kind of roundness. I found that I was expressing admiration of her points as if she were some kind of museum piece, and that she seemed to enjoy being posed in the setting of the fresh rose sheath, as if some frank and unashamed self-complacency coexisted with her morbid self-doubt. "I have too much flesh on my stomach," she said, and, "I know you don't approve of stained toenails—but I like them": she had colored them red. But what struck and astonished me most was that not

only were her thighs perfect columns but that all that lay between them was impressively beautiful, too, with an ideal aesthetic value that I had never found there before. The mount was of a classical femininity: round and smooth and plump; the fleece, if not quite golden, was blond and curly and soft; and the portals were a deep tender rose, like the petals of some fleshly flower. And they were doing their feminine work of making things easy for the entrant with a honeysweet sleek profusion that showed I had quite misjudged her in suspecting as I had sometimes done that she was really unresponsive to caresses. She became, in fact, so smooth and open that after a moment I could hardly feel her. Her little bud was so deeply embedded that it was hardly involved in the play, and she made me arrest my movement while she did something special and gentle that did not, however, press on this point, rubbing herself somehow against me—and then consummated, with a self-excited tremor that appeared to me curiously mild for a woman of her positive energy. I went on and had a certain disappointment, for, with the brimming of female fluid, I felt even less sensation; but—gently enough—I came, too.

Q. Now, do you feel that that type of writing adds to the literary merit of a book?

Trilling: That is a difficult question to answer. If I had to answer it yes or no, I would say yes; not making an abstract principle, of "that kind of writing," because I don't quite know how you are characterizing "that kind of writing." If you would characterize it as a rather precise and literal account of a woman's sexual parts in the sexual act, and if you would go on to admit that the story is about sexuality, then I would say yes, it added to the accuracy, precision of the story.

Q. Well, I will read another part [Reads passage from pp. 210–11]:

I remember one cold winter Sunday when she had come in the afternoon, a day of blank uptown facades and decorous uptown perspectives, when I had gone to the deserted museum to look something up in a book, and, returning, I had felt it so incongruous to watch her take off her stiff pink slip and to have her in her prosaic brassiere: the warm and adhesive body and the mossy damp underparts—the mystery, the organic animal, the prime human oven of heat and juice—between the cold afternoon sheets in the gray-lit Sunday room; and one evening when I had come home from a party at which I made Imogen smile by my tender and charming gallantries and kissed her hand at parting, and then made love to Anna for the second time, by a sudden revival of appetite after she had put on her clothes to go, by way of her white thighs and buttocks, laid bare between black dress and gray stockings—she was so slim that it was almost as easy to take her from behind as face to face—while she kicked up one foot in its blunt-toed black shoe as a gesture of playful resistance or simply of wanton freedom.

Q. Now, do you think it is necessary to describe people's movements and parts of sex organs to make a book a great book?

Trilling: Literary necessity is very hard to define. In a certain sense, nothing is necessary and everything is necessary. What is necessary is what it is that will give the effect that the writer intends. Here, I take it, he wants to contrast his vulgar—what is outspoken—with what he is calling "tender and charming gallantry," and his point can't quite be made, perhaps, unless he put one thing against another.

Q. Do you think the great books of literature, the great love stories, say, *Scarlet Letter*, have suffered because they haven't had a detailed description of sex acts and sex organs?

Trilling: I don't quite think this is a love story. I think this is a story of sexuality, which is a different thing.

Q. I have no further questions.

A ludicrous and unsuccessful trial which merely served to give the book a much-welcomed publicity boost.

And quite a marvelous new approach: not a love story, but one of sexuality.

13

Ugh, E-e-e-uuu, and Gross

I shall be back in two weeks
to embrace you passionately. Do not bathe.
N. Bonaparte in a letter to Josephine

Y EARS AGO, MY OLD FRIEND, AUTHOR SLOAN WILSON (*THE MAN in the Gray Flannel Suit*, etc.), cautioned me:

"If you've written a sex scene and it doesn't make the reader want to do what they're doing—whatever it is—you haven't written it right."

Sounded good at the time. Yet, I have encountered so many sex scenes in novels which recount activities that I not only don't want to emulate myself, but about which I don't even want to read and which diminish the book for me.

For an example of a scene I don't care to re-visit or even quote here, the villain's idea of fun in James Paterson's best-selling second Alex Cross novel, *Kill the Girls*, where he feeds a live snake into the anus of one of his female victims.

The reader of this book may wish to skip this whole chapter even though the excerpts come from mainstream, Book-of-the-Month-type writers, with their best-selling novels.

In the last chapter, we looked at an excerpt from a Norman Mailer book. Here's another excerpt from the same book, *The Time of Our Time* (1959), an unlovely and unloving and un-sexy scene:

As I started to slip up her sweater, she got away and said a little huskily, "I'll take my own clothes off." Once again I could have hit her. My third eye, that athlete's inner eye which probed its vision into all the corners, happy and distressed of my body whole, was glumly cautioning the congestion of the spirits in the coils of each teste. They would have to wait, turn rancid, maybe die of delay.

Off came the sweater and the needless brassiere, her economical breasts swelled just a trifle tonight, enough to take on the convexities of an Amazon's armor. Open came the belt and the zipper of her dungarees, zipped from the front which pleased her not a little. Only her ass, a small masterpiece, and her strong thighs, justified this theater. She stood there naked, quite psychicly clothed, and lit a cigarette.

If a stiff prick has no conscience, it has also no common sense. I stood there like a clown, trying to coax her to take a ride with me on the bawdy car, she out of her clothes, I in all of mine, a muscular little mermaid to melt on my knee. She laughed, one harsh banker's snort—she was giving no loans on my idiot's collateral.

"You didn't even ask me," Denise thought to say, "of how my studying went tonight."

"What did you study?"

"I didn't. I didn't study." She gave me a lovely smile, girlish and bright. "I just spent the last three hours with Arthur."

"You're a dainty type," I told her.

But she gave me a bad moment. That lovely flesh-spent smell, scent of the well-used and the tender, that avatar of the feminine my senses had accepted so greedily, came down now to no more than the rubbings and the sweats of what was probably a very nice guy, passive Arthur with his Jewish bonanzas of mouth-love.

The worst of it was that it quickened me more. I had the selfish wisdom to throw such evidence upon the mercy of my own court. For the smell of Arthur was the smell of love, at least for me, and so from man or woman, it did not matter—the smell of love was always feminine—and if the man in Denise was melted by the woman in Arthur, so Arthur might have flowered that woman in himself from the arts of a real woman, his mother?—it did not matter—that voiceless message which passed from the sword of the man into the cavern of the woman was carried along from body to body, and if it was not the woman in Denise I was going to find tonight, at least I would be warmed by the previous trace of another.

But that was a tone poem to quiet the toads of my doubt. When Denise—it took five more minutes—finally decided to expose herself on my clumped old mattress, the sight of her black pubic hair, the feel of the foreign but brotherly liquids in her un-embarrassed maw, turned me into a jackrabbit of pissy tumescence, the quicks of my excitement beheaded from the resonances of my body, and I wasn't with her a half-minute before I was over, gone, and off. I rode not with the strength to reap the harem of her and her lover, but spit like a pinched little boy up into black forested hills of motherly contempt, a passing picture of the nuns of my childhood to drench my piddle spurtings with failures of gloom. She it was who proved stronger than me, she the he to my silly she.

All considered, Denise was nice about it. Her harsh laugh did not crackle over my head, her hand in passing me the after-cigarette settled for no more than a nudge of my nose, and if it were not for the contempt of her tough grin, I would have been left with no more than the alarm to the sweepers of my brain to sweep this failure away.

"Hasn't happened in years," I said to her, the confession coming out of me with the cost of the hardest cash.

"Oh, shut up. Just rest." And she began to hum a mocking little song.

Awfully wordy and not appealing to the reader, and most unforgivable of all, not important to the characters, hence not important to the story.

A weird, and to my mind, his most unimportant novel, is Ernest Hemingway's book, *Garden of Eden*, published twenty-five years after his death. It is mostly about sex. Here's one of the tamer scenes:

He heard the Bugatti come up the long slope and turn onto the gravel and stop.

Catherine came into the room. She had a scarf over her head and sunglasses on and she took them off and kissed David. He held her close and said, "How are you?"

"Not so good," she said. "It was too hot." She smiled at him and put her forehead on his shoulder. "I'm glad I'm home."

He went out and made a Tom Collins and brought it in to Catherine who had finished a cold shower. She took the tall cold glass and sipped from it and then held it against the smooth dark skin of her belly. She touched the glass to the ups of each of her breasts so they came erect and then took a long sip and held the cold glass against her belly again. "This is wonderful," she said.

He kissed her and she said, "Oh, that's nice. I'd forgotten about that. I don't see any good reason why I should give that up. Do you?"

"No."

"Well, I haven't," she said. "I'm not going to turn you over to someone else prematurely. That was a silly idea."

"Get dressed and come on out," David said.

"No. I want to have fun with you like in the old days."

"How?"

"You know. To make you happy."

"How happy?"

"This."

"Be careful," he said.

"Please."

"All right, if you want."

"The way it was in Grau du Roi the first time it ever happened?"

"If you want."

"Thank you for giving me this time because—"

"Don't talk."

"It's just like Grau du Roi but it's lovelier because it's in the daytime and we love each other more because I'd gone away. Please let's be slow and slow and slow—"

"Yes slow."

"Are you—"

"Yes."

"Are you really?"

"Yes, if you want."

"Oh I want so much and you are and I have. Please be slow and let me keep it."

"You have it."

"Yes I do. I do have it. Oh, yes, I do. I do. Please come now with me. Please can you now—"

They lay on the sheets and Catherine with her brown leg over his, touching his instep lightly with her toes, rested on her elbows and lifted her mouth from his and said, "Are you glad to have me back?"

"You," he said. "You did come back."

It *does* sound a bit like a college humor magazine's parody of Hemingway. There are ugh-making scenes where the lovers switch gender roles and experiment—but why bother? You don't want to know.

For some seventeen years, a group in Britain called the Bad Sex in Fiction have awarded prizes "celebrating" crude, tasteless, or ridiculous sexual passages in modern literature. The judges, editors of *Literary Review* magazine, say that John Updike has been short-listed for the prize four times over the years. Three years ago, his novel, *The Widows of Eastwick*, took second place, the awarded scene being "a description of an explosive oral encounter." Updike likes oral and anal encounters a lot.

Author Katie Roiphe wrote the following commentary in the *New York Times* in January of 2010:

> In *Couples*, a graphic description of oral sex includes "the floral surfaces of her mouth." In *Rabbit, Run*, we read of "lovely wobbly bubbles, heavy: perfume between. Taste, salt and sour, swirls back with his own saliva." The hallmark of Updike's sex scenes is the mingling of his usual brutal realism with a stepped-up rapture, a harsh scrutiny combined with prettiness. Everything is rose, milky, lilac, and then suddenly it is not.
>
> For Rabbit, as with many Updike characters, sex offers an escape, an alternate life—a reprieve, even, in its finest moments, from mortality.

Here's some dialogue from Updike's novel, *Couples*:

> "Have you ever slept with anyone except Piet?"
> "Never. I thought maybe I should."
> "Why?"

"So I'd be better at it."

"For *him*. Shit. Let's face it, Angela. You married a bastard. A bully boy. He's pimping for you. He's got you so intimidated you'll shack up with anybody he tells you to."

"You're not anybody, Freddy. I more or less trust you. You're like me. You want to teach."

"I used to. Then I learned the final thing to teach and I didn't want to learn any more."

"What final thing?"

"We die. We don't die for one second out there in the future, we die all the time, in every direction. Every meal we eat breaks down the enamel."

"Hey. You've gotten bigger."

"Death excites me. Death is being screwed by God. It'll be delicious."

"You don't believe in God."

"I believe in that one, Big Man Death. I smell Him between people's teeth every day."

He was hoping to keep her at a distance with such violence of vision but she nudged closer again, crowding him with formless warmth. Her toes engaged his toes; her chin dug into his chest, the hard bone to the right of the heart. "Piet's terrified of death," she said, snuggling.

Freddy told her, "It's become his style. He uses it now as self-justification. He's mad at the world for killing his parents."

"Men are so romantic," Angela said, after waiting for him to tell her more. "Piet spends all his energy defying death, and you spend all yours accepting it."

"That's the difference between us. Male versus female."

"You think of yourself as female?"

"Of course. Clearly I'm homosexual. But then, of the men in town, who isn't, except poor old Piet?"

"Freddy. You're just leading me on, to see what I'll say. Be sincere."

"I am sincere. Anybody with a little psychology can see I'm right. Think. Frank and Harold. They screw each other's wives because they're too snobbish to screw each other. Janet senses it;

she's just their excuse. Take Guerin and Constantine. They're made for each other."

"Of course, Roger—"

"Eddie's worse. He's a successful sadist. Or Gallagher and Whitman. Spoiled priests. Saltz and Ong, maybe not, but one's moving and the other's dying. Anyway, they don't count, they're not Christian. Me, I'm worst of all, I want to be everybody's mother. I want to have breasts so everybody can have a suck. Why do you think I drink so much? To make milk."

Angela said, "You've really thought about this, haven't you?"

"No, I'm making it all up, to distract your attention from my limp prick; but it works, doesn't it? Piet stands alone. No wonder the women in town are tearing him to pieces."

"Is that why you've always hated him?"

"Hated him, hell. I love him. We both love him."

"Freddy, you are not a homosexual and I'm going to prove it." She pushed herself higher in bed, so her breasts swam into starlight and her pelvis was above his. She lifted a thigh so it rested on his hipbone. "Come on. Put it in me."

He had kept a half-measure of firmness, but the slick warmth of her vagina singed him like a finger too slowly passed through a candle flame.

Feeling him grow little again, she asked again, "What can I do?"

He suggested, "Blow me?"

"Do what? I don't know how."

Pitying her, seeing through this confession into a mansion of innocence that the Hanemas, twin closed portals, had concealed, Freddy said, "Skip it. Let's gossip. Tell me if you think Janet still goes to bed with Harold."

"She made a big deal of getting cottages at opposite ends of the row."

"Merely thirty or so yards, not very far even in bare feet, if your heart's in it."

I think we can assume that not much is going to come from this particular coupling. To sum things up, in commenting on John Updike's writing about sex, some wit once quipped, "John's a penis with a thesaurus."

I have always found Henry Miller to be gross, and unbearably crude, but at one point everyone in America read his two most famous books, *Tropic of Cancer* and *Tropic of Capricorn*. The following is a sample from the latter book:

What about that red-haired girl in SU office...you remember... the one with the big teats? Wasn't that a nice piece of ass to turn over to a friend? But I did it, didn't I? I did it because you said you liked big teats. But I wouldn't do it for Curley. He's a little crook. Let him do his own digging.

As a matter of fact, Curley was digging away very industri- ously. He must have had five or six on the string at one time, from what I could gather. There was Valeska, for example—he had made himself pretty solid with her. She was so damned pleased to have some one fuck her without blushing that when it came to shar- ing him with her cousin and then with the midget she didn't put up the least objection. What she liked best was to get in the tub and let him fuck her under water. It was fine until the midget got wise to it. Then there was a nice rumpus which was finally ironed out on the parlor floor. To listen to Curley talk he did everything but climb the chandeliers. And always plenty of pocket money to boot. Valeska was generous, but the cousin was a softy. If she came within a foot of a stiff prick she was like putty. An unbuttoned fly was enough to put her in a trance. It was almost shameful the things Curley made her do. He took pleasure in degrading her. I could scarcely blame him for it, she was such a prim, priggish bitch in her street clothes. You'd almost swear she didn't own a cunt, the way she carried herself in the street. Naturally, when he got her alone he made her pay for her highfalutin' ways. He went at it cold-bloodedly. "Fish it out!" he'd say, opening his fly a little. "Fish it out with your tongue!" (He had it in for the whole bunch because, as he put it, they were sucking one another off behind his back.) Anyway, once she got the taste of it in her mouth you could do anything with her. Sometimes he'd stand her on her hands and push her around the room that way, like a wheelbarrow. Or else he'd do it dog fashion, and while she groaned and squirmed he'd nonchalantly light a cigarette and blow the smoke between her legs. Once he played her a dirty trick doing it that way. He had worked her up to such a state that she was beside herself. Anyway, after he had almost polished the ass off her with his back-scuttling he pulled out for a second, as though to cool his cock off, and then very slowly and gently he shoved a big long carrot up her twat. "That, Miss Abercrombie," he said, "is a sort of Doppelganger to my regular cock," and with that he unhitches himself and yanks up his pants. Cousin Abercrombie was so bewildered by it all that she let a tremendous fart and out tumbled the carrot. At least, that's how Curley related it to me. He was an outrageous liar, to be sure, and there may not be a grain of truth in the yarn, but there's no denying that he had a flair for such tricks. As for Miss Abercrombie and her high-tone Narragansett ways, well, with a cunt like that, one can always imagine the worst. By comparison Hymie was a purist. Somehow Hymie and his fat circumcised dick were two different things. When he got a personal hard on, as he said, he really meant that he was irresponsible. He meant that Nature was asserting itself—through his, Hymie Laubscher's, fat circumcised dick. It was the same with his wife's cunt. It was something she wore between her legs, like an ornament. It was a part of Mrs. Laubscher but it wasn't Mrs. Laubscher personally, if you get what I mean.

Well, all this is simply by way of leading up to the general sexual confusion which prevailed at this time. It was like taking a flat in the Land of Fuck.

The girl upstairs, for instance...

— and on and on, one pointless sexual situation after another.

But as Ezra Pound said about Henry Miller: "At last, a printable book that is readable."

Chaque un a son goût.

(Ezra Pound ended up in an asylum for the—er—unbalanced.)

Yes, Miller's sex books are readable, but so is *Hustler* magazine. In all fairness, Miller wrote a couple of books that were beautifully written—and contain no sexual scenes whatsoever.

Taken from her 2001 collection of stories, *Faithless—Tales of Transgression*, the following is an excerpt from Joyce Carol Oates's story, "What Then, My Life?"

From out of nowhere in front of me, there was my cousin
Luke. He'd run ahead of me to cut me off, chunky yellowish teeth
bared in a dog's grin, but I scrambled sideways, I was quick and
crazed as a wild, hunted animal, but behind me there was another
boy—shirtless, his skinny dark chest sleek with sweat, and for a
moment I believed this was a third boy, a stranger, not Jake, my
cousin Jake, but of course it was Jake, though his dirty grinning
face wasn't a face I seemed to recognize, and his clownish pop-
eyes. And there was Luke's flushed face, his laughing teeth, his
angry teeth, why was he angry, and that sharp frown between his
eyebrows like a knife blade the way an adult man might frown, the
way my father frowned when one of his children displeased him,
that staring frown of wrath. Luke grabbed at me but was able to
catch only my T-shirt, the neck and the sleeve of my T-shirt he
ripped, I was swinging my fists at his middle, at his chest, we were
on the ground wrestling, crashing against the brittle cornstalks,
dried corncobs hard and hurting beneath my back, my bottom,
Luke grunted, cursing me, straddling me, holding me tight as
a vise with his thighs, he was tickling me with something hard
and scratchy, something his fingers had closed over, and Jake was
crouched over us panting, cursing, yet happy, tugging at one of my
ankles, tugging at my shorts which he managed to yank down only
a few inches before his way was stopped by Luke's tight-pressed
knee. I smelled the strong animal sweat on their bodies. I smelled
my own suddenly released hot pee, I screamed and kicked Jake
in the belly, between the legs so he whimpered in pain, Luke was
laughing wildly, tickling—poking at me with that hard scratchy
object, I didn't see it, I don't believe I saw it, only the confused
recollection afterward of an object consisting of hundreds of tiny
eyes, except the crows had pecked away most of the eyes, there were
rows of tiny gouged-out eyes, it was hurting me, under my arms,
my tummy, between my legs, between the cheeks of my buttocks
where I was tender, where I could bleed, I was kicking, squealing,
except Luke had pressed his salty-sweaty palm over my mouth to
shut me up, his face was strained like a fist clenched tight, his jaws
were clenched tight, I saw his eyes rolling white and I screamed
through the hard hurting flat of his hand, and in that instant the
earth opened up, it was a black soft-melting pit into which I fell,

like falling asleep in church, my head pitching forward suddenly, the cornfield was still bright with light, dazzling and blinding with light, and the patches of sky overhead, but I wasn't there to see, my boy cousins grunting and cursing but I wasn't there to hear.

Shades of Faulkner's *Sanctuary*—what is it about corncobs?

Harry Crews is the tough-writing, ex-Marine author of a dozen novels, the best known probably *A Feast of Snakes*. In his short story "Carny," he offers up this bit of unattractive American carnival lore:

After the first show was over and they had made us lighter by $3, things happened quickly. Peeling the eggs took the longest. But first they added a drummer to the act. Really, a drummer. The ladies had retired behind a rat-colored curtain and out onto the little platform came an old man dressed in an ancient blue suit with a blue cap that at first I thought belonged to the Salvation Army. And it may have. Ligaments stood in his scrawny neck like wire. He sat on a chair and put his bass drum between his legs. The caller started the record we had already heard twice, which, incidentally, was by Frankie Valli, and the old man started pounding on his drum. His false teeth bulged in his old mouth every time he struck it. Never once during the performance did he look up. I know he did not see Rose. I was fascinated that he would not look at her when she came out onto the stage. She was naked except for a halter. I swear. She had her tits cinched up, but there was her old naked beaver and strong, over-the-hill ass. She was carrying six eggs in a little bowl. She carried it just the way a whore would have carried a bowl, except she had eggs in it instead of soap and water. She squatted in front of us—taking us all the way to pink—while she peeled the eggs. When they were peeled, she placed them one by one in her mouth, slobbered on them good and returned them to the dish. Then, still squatting, with Frankie Valli squealing for all he was worth and the old man single-mindedly beating his drum, and several of the good old boys hugging each other, she popped all of the eggs into her pussy and started dancing. She did six high kicks in her dance and each time she kicked, she fired an egg with considerable velocity out into the audience. On a bet with his buddies, a young apprentice madman caught and ate the last two.

I left the tent disappointed, though. I'd seen the act before. Once, many years ago, I knew a lady in New Orleans who could do a dozen. Not a dozen of your grade-A extra-large, to be sure. They were smalls, but a dozen nonetheless.

It's unclear exactly when proctology invaded polite literature, but it found its champions quickly enough in Updike, Roth, and many others.

The following is an excerpt from a 1974 novel, *The Black House*, by Paul Theroux, and, yes, he's the same Theroux who wrote the marvelous travel books. Alfred Munday loves Caroline but he is married to Emma. No matter. She is asleep upstairs when he takes Caroline into his house.

Munday said, "It's wrong—us here."

Caroline fed the fire. It crackled, louder than her voice as she whispered, "Don't you see? This is the only place it's right."

"She's sleeping," said Munday, after a moment.

"Ah," said Caroline, and smiled, but Munday was not sure whether she was smiling at what he had just said or at the fire, which she stacked with larger pieces of split wood. It was roaring in the chimney now, and the air moved in the room, larger and much brighter with the tall candles and the sticks alight.

"We'll wake her," Munday said in a voice so small it was as if he had spoken something pointless to himself. He looked at Caroline; she was barefoot, she still crouched, her buttocks on her heels; she was naked under her dress, and her breasts swung as she worked with the fire.

"Then don't talk," she said. He was fascinated by the way she attended to the fire. It reddened her skin, and standing above her and a little to the side he could see through the sleeveless opening in her dress and the long open collar, the snout of one breast with its fire-lit foraging nipple. For the first time since he had entered the room she moved her shoulders and looked up at him. "Why are you wearing that coat?"

She lunged for it and snatched the edge of it and drew him down beside her, making him drop to his knees. Wriggling, she shook out of the top of her dress and pushed it down her arms and worked it to her waist with her thumbs. She left it there, bunched under her white stomach that jutted forward as she kneeled. She was half naked, in a sarong. Munday watched her, too startled to move, and he saw in her breasts and belly and navel a body mask, the shape of a face, with nipples for eyes, the kind Africans sometimes carved for erotic dances. But theirs were ebony and this was white, the stark face of a willing girl-woman, given expression by the moving shadow of the fire, a plea hatching from her eye-sockets beseeching him to kiss. Then he was tasting it; it was caressing his tongue. Caroline had reached for his head, and with one hand behind his neck and the other under her breast, she lifted her breast into his face. Munday nuzzled the tender orbit of the nipple while she held the breast in her fingers, offering it like fruit...

The ceiling swam with mottled firelight, and Munday caressed Caroline's legs, the backs of her thighs, and pushed the silken folds of her long skirt aside, unveiling the cool yellow-white globes of her buttocks. She straddled him, facing away, butting his chest with her knees as she crossed over, and still moving her head and making devouring gasps on his penis, she settled on him and moved her cunt against his face. Munday held loosely to her skirt and received her with his tongue, lapping the slickness of her vulva's lips. He was drowning, smothering pleasurably in fathoms of swamp, the ferns prickling his chin, his mouth teased by a pouring tide of eels and damp spiney plant-roots. His arms were helpless, his hands light, falling away from flotsam that dissolved in his grasp. Caroline moved slightly, thrusting down, and Munday licked the seam in the groove that ran to where her arse budded. She groaned and pitched forward, her face against the floor. "Yes, yes," Munday parted her buttocks and licked at the rough pebbles of the bud. He warmed it, and it opened like a flower on his mouth; he darted his tongue into it, deliriously urged by her moanings. His skin burned from the fire, it seared his arms, and the side of Caroline closest to the fire was hot to the touch, hot enough for him to imagine her skin peeling from her flesh. This heat and her muffled sobs drove him on, and he ignored the fracture in his heart and licked at her in a greedy frenzy for her approval, until her sobs turned to soft howls of pleasure.

Katie Roiphe recently wrote in the the *New York Times* about Philip
Roth's works:

> Part of the suspense of a Roth passage, the tautness, the
> brilliance, the bravado in the sentences themselves, the high-wire
> performance of his prose, is how infuriating and ugly and vain he
> can be without losing his readers (and then every now and then
> he actually goes ahead and loses them).

Let's end this chapter with a typical Roth scene. Well, maybe there's
no such thing as a *typical* Roth scene.

This is from his 2009 novel, *The Humbling*:

> The pain from the spinal condition made it impossible for
> him to fuck her from above or even from the side, and so he lay
> on his back and she mounted him supporting herself on her knees
> and her hands so as not to lower her weight onto his pelvis. At
> first she lost all her know-how up there and he had to guide her
> with his two hands to give her the idea. "I don't know what to do,"
> Pegeen said shyly. "You're on a horse," Axler told her. "Ride it."
> When he worked his thumb into her ass she sighed with pleasure
> and whispered, "Nobody's ever put anything in there before"—
> "Unlikely," he whispered back—and when later he put his cock in
> there, she took as much as she could of it until she couldn't take
> any more. "Did it hurt?" he asked her. "It hurt, but it's you." Often
> she would hold his cock in her palm afterward and stare as the
> erection subsided. "What are you contemplating?" he asked. "It
> fills you up," she said, "the way dildos and fingers don't. It's alive.
> It's a living thing." She quickly mastered riding the horse, and soon
> while she worked slowly up and down she began to say, "Hit me,"
> and when he hit her, she said mockingly, "Is that as hard as you
> can do it?" "Your face is already red." "Harder," she said. "Okay,
> but why?" "Because I've given you permission to do it. Because it
> hurts. Because it makes me feel like a little girl and it makes me
> feel like a whore. Go ahead. Harder."
>   She had a small plastic bag of sex toys that she brought with
> her one weekend, spilled them out on the sheets when they were
> getting ready for bed. He'd seen his share of dildos, but never, other

than in pictures, the strap-on leather harness that held the dildo secure and enabled one woman to mount and penetrate another. He'd asked her to bring her toys with her, and now he watched as she pulled the harness over her thighs and on up to her hips, where she tightened it like a belt. She looked like a gunslinger getting dressed, a gunslinger with a swagger. Then she inserted a green rubber dildo into a slot in the harness that was just about level with her clitoris. She stood alongside the bed wearing only that. "Let me see yours," she said. He removed his pants and threw them over the side of the bed while she grabbed the green cock and, having lubricated it first with baby oil, pretended to masturbate like a man. Admiringly he said, "It looks authentic." "You want me to fuck you with it." "No, thanks," he said. "I wouldn't hurt you," she said cajolingly, kittenishly lowering her voice. "I promise to be very gentle with you," she said. "Funny, but you don't look like you'll be gentle." "You mustn't be deceived by appearances. Oh, let me," she said, laughing, "you'll *like* it. It's a new frontier." *"You'll* like it. No, I'd prefer you to suck me off," he said. "While I wear my cock," she said. "Yes." "While I wear my big thick green cock." "That's what I want." "While I wear my big green cock and you play with my tits." "That sounds right." "And after I suck you off," she said, "you'll suck me off. You'll go down on my big green cock." "I could do that," he said.

Etcetera, etcetera, truly *ad nauseum.*

As the Spaniards say—*"Entre qustos y colores, no hay disputas, señores."* Which translates roughly into: "You can't argue with anyone about taste or color preferences."

Or sex scenes.

I believe a good way to remove the bad taste from some of the scenes in this book would be to read—or re-read—the great love and sex story by Anton Chekov called "The Lady With the Dog." It is moving, wrenching, and romantic, but totally tasteful and convincing. A great antidote, it will renew your faith in the possibility of writing about this fundamental human activity in a powerful but inoffensive way. It is too good and totally of a single-piece to violate by excerpting any part of it.

Conclusion

Dickens says that writers must be actors; they must be the players in their stories, must act out the scenes in their heads.

This is especially true of the writing of sex scenes. But before actually writing a sex scene, ask yourself a few things:

Do I really need a sex scene in this story? Despite William F. Buckley's calling them "the obligatory sex scene[s]," it is not really obligatory unless your name is Henry Miller or Jackie Collins. Think of the countless distinguished writers who have written of *love* but never included sex scenes in their books: Dickens, Kipling, Twain, Chekov, London, Michener, etcetera, etcetera.

I don't think anything I've read about whether one should or shouldn't write "*that* scene" is as good as the following paragraph by Steve Alcorn from an essay called "How To Write Sex Scenes, The 12-Step Program":

> If you don't feel comfortable writing about sex, then don't. By this, I mean writing about sex as it actually exists, in the real world, as an ecstatic, terrifying, and, above all, deeply emotional process. Real sex is compelling to read about because the participants are so utterly vulnerable. We are all, when the time comes to get naked, terribly excited and frightened and hopeful and doubtful, usually all at the same time. You mustn't abandon your characters in their time of need. You mustn't make of them naked playthings with rubbery parts. You must love them, wholly and without shame, as

they go about their human business. Because we've already got a name for sex without emotional content: pornography.

If you do decide to include a graphic sexual scene, ask yourself a few questions:

Is the language used by the characters true to what we know about them and their backgrounds?

In other words, does the man talk like Marlon Brando or does he sound like Noel Coward? Does the woman use words that Judy O'Grady would use or rather more like the Colonel's lady's vocabulary? They may be "sisters under the skin," but they don't sound the same.

At orgasm, does she whisper a lady-like "Yes, yes!" —or does she scream "It's Howdy Doody time!"

And, what words are appropriate for the author himself or herself to use when describing this or that intimate activity?

At whom are you aiming this particular scene and what effect will it have on the reader? It is very easy to lose a reader's affection and interest in a character if he or she behaves in what the reader perceives to be bad or crude or brutal conduct in a sex scene.

This book is intended mainly as a help to writers to decide which way they're going to jump when their characters start to lust after each other. But I also hope it has revelatory moments for readers who enjoy great writing: In the year and a half I have worked on this book, I often would get a recommended book from the library, turn to the sex scene, get hooked by the good writing, and spend the next two days reading every word of the novel. I wanted to find out what the characters did with their time *out* of bed. I must have read at least 150 entire books, and I regretted not a moment. I either re-discovered old friends, or was disillusioned by some, or found splendid new ones. Perhaps some readers, intrigued by an excerpt herein, will be motivated to go seek the whole book in the library nearest them. Everyone quoted in this book is in there—and they aren't declared obscene or wrapped in brown paper or placed in a special section.

I would like to leave you with some deathless words and rigid rules about the writings of sex scenes, but the best I can do is to quote William Shakespeare, that English writer who talked funny and in clichés and never wrote a graphic sex scene in his life:

"To thine own self be true..."

If you write a sex scene that offends you, it will surely offend some others, and maybe that is what your story calls for. And, conversely, if you write a sex scene that comes from the heart or memory or the libido, it will most likely please others and do the job you intended.

And, as long as we're quoting English writers, we can well end this book by quoting poet Andrew Marvell's immortal lines from "To His Coy Mistress."

> "The grave's a fine and private place,
> But none I think do there embrace."

Those golden, soothing words from so many centuries ago might be the single most successful, seductive pick-up line ever written.

Index

More by BARNABY CONRAD

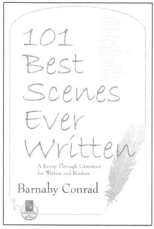

$14.95 US

101 Best Scenes Ever Written
A Romp Through Literature for Writers and Readers
—by Barnaby Conrad

    Here in one volume you will find beloved scenes you read in the past, or perhaps great scenes you had forgotten, or totally new scenes to be discovered and savored. Any reader will enjoy browsing Barnaby Conrad's choices of the greatest scenes ever written, but the real beneficiaries of this book will be the countless fledgling writers who will learn by sampling and studying these gems from the masters of the written word.

> **❝** A superb book! Indispensable! Get it! **❞**
> —Ray Bradbury, author of *The Martian Chronicles*

$15.95 US

101 Best Beginnings Ever Written
A Romp Through Literary Openings for Writers and Readers
—by Barnaby Conrad

    For writers and readers, the first part of every story is the most important. Bestselling author Barnaby Conrad identifies the twelve types of beginnings, teaching writers how to start their stories with forceful, compelling prose that hooks their readers from page one.

> **❝** A book as wise and companionable as its author, and a superb resource for writer, student and literary bystander alike. Bravo! Olé! **❞**
> —Christopher Buckley, author of *Thank You for Smoking*

Available from bookstores, online bookstores, and QuillDriverBooks.com, or by calling toll-free 1-800-345-4447.

Practical books for working writers

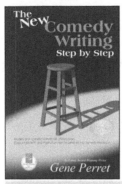

More great books for writers

Write Your Book Now!
A proven system to start and FINISH the book you've always wanted to write!

——*by Emmy Award-winning writer Gene Perret*

Whether you aspire to write a romance, an expert guide to business success, or the Great American Novel, *Write Your Book Now!* gives you proven, field-tested tools to successfully finish the book you've always wanted to write. *Write Your Book Now!* simplifies the book-writing project by breaking it down into a series of discrete tasks anyone can accomplish. Emmy Award-winner Gene Perret helps you avoid distractions and delays, combat your emotional blocks, and establish and maintain a powerful writing momentum up to completion.

Books, Crooks and Counselors
How to Write Accurately About Criminal Law and Courtroom Procedure

—*by Leslie Budewitz*, mystery writer and attorney at law

Whether you write murder mysteries, suspense thrillers, or courtroom dramas, you want to get it right when using legal concepts and terminology or depicting courtroom procedure. *Books, Crooks and Counselors* is an easy-to-use, practical, and reliable guidebook that shows writers how to use the law to create fiction that is accurate, true-to-life, and crackling with real-world tension and conflict. Leslie Budewitz, a practicing lawyer (and mystery writer) with over 25 years of courtroom experience, will teach you the facts of legal procedure, what lawyers and judges really think about the law, and authentic courtroom dialogue.

Writing advice from an author/shrink

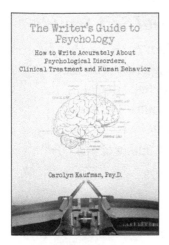

The Writer's Guide to
Psychology

How to Write Accurately About
Psychological Disorders,
Clinical Treatment and Human Behavior

Carolyn Kaufman, Psy.D.

$14.95 US)

DON'T LET THIS HAPPEN TO YOU!

In *New Moon*, the follow-up to Stephenie Meyer's bestselling novel *Twilight*, the author repeatedly confuses hallucinations with delusions, using the two words interchangeably. "I was addicted to the sound of my delusions," the heroine, Bella, says. This is impossible, since delusions are ideas or beliefs. Hearing voices and seeing things both fall into the category of hallucinations.

The Writer's Guide to Psychology
How to Write Accurately About Psychological Disorders, Clinical Treatment and Human Behavior
—by Carolyn Kaufman, Psy.D.

Writers frequently write about mental illness and psychological motivations, but all too often they use terms and concepts that are clichéd, outmoded or just plain wrong.

Written by a clinical psychologist who is also a professional writer and writing coach, *The Writer's Guide to Psychology* is an authoritative, accessible, fun, and easy-to-use reference to psychological disorders, diagnosis, treatments, psychotherapists' work and what really makes psychopathic villains tick.

The only reference book on psychology designed specifically for writers, *The Writer's Guide to Psychology* presents specific writing dos and don'ts to avoid the psychobabble clichés and misunderstandings frequently seen in popular writing. The book's extensive sidebars include "Don't Let This Happen to You!" boxes that humorously expose mortifying mistakes in fiction, film and TV … and teach readers how to get it right in their own writing.

The Writer's Guide to Psychology is a unique combination of accurate psychology, myth-busting information and practical guidance that belongs on every writer's reference shelf.

❝ This book should be in every writer's professional library and every clinician's, too — whether writers or not!❞

—New York Journal of Books

Available from bookstores, online bookstores, and QuillDriverBooks.com, or by calling toll-free 1-800-345-4447.

Yes, You Can Make Money as a Writer